A GIFT FOR:

....

FROM:

....

DATE:

....

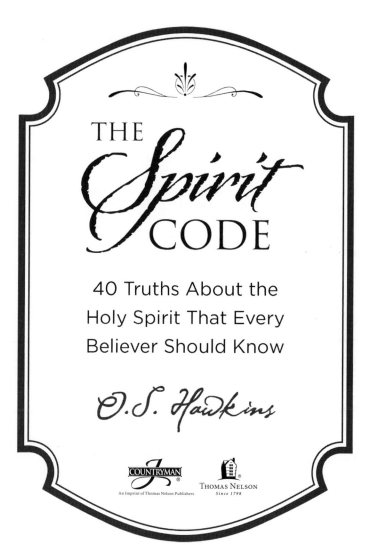

THE

Spirit

CODE

40 Truths About the
Holy Spirit That Every
Believer Should Know

O. S. Hawkins

COUNTRYMAN®

An Imprint of Thomas Nelson Publishers

THOMAS NELSON
Since 1798

The Spirit Code
© 2024 Dr. O. S. Hawkins

Published in Nashville, Tennessee, by Thomas Nelson. Thomas Nelson is a registered trademark of HarperCollins Christian Publishing, Inc.

Thomas Nelson titles may be purchased in bulk for educational, business, fundraising, or sales promotional use. For information, please email SpecialMarkets@ThomasNelson.com.

Cover design by Bruce DeRoos, Left Coast Design, LLC
Interior design by Kristy L. Edwards

ISBN 978-1-4002-4643-4 (HC)
ISBN 978-1-4002-4659-5 (audiobook)
ISBN 978-1-4002-4657-1 (eBook)

Printed in India

24 25 26 27 28 TPI 10 9 8 7 6 5 4 3 2 1

CONTENTS

INTRODUCTION

One of the saddest verses to be found in all the Bible is in the aftermath of Jesus' arrest in Gethsemane's garden one dark night. Of the apostles, the Bible simply records, "They all forsook Him and fled" (Mark 14:50). Just hours before, back in the upper room, they had been so sure of themselves, so bold, so boastful of their loyalty to Him in the face of any kind of opposition. But then, when it came down to the crisis moment, when all was on the line, they ran away. They went AWOL. They took flight into the darkness when they were needed the most.

Fast-forward a few days. Look at Simon Peter. He had denied knowing the Lord three distinct times that fateful evening of the arrest, even cursing as he sat in Caiaphas's courtyard, warming to the fire—while Jesus was beaten and being held in a dungeon just a few yards away. But the transformation that would soon take place in his life is astounding. Later, after being imprisoned himself, beaten and commanded by the authorities never to speak in the name of Jesus again, he stood up to his full height, looked his tormentors square in the eyes, and said, "We cannot but speak the things which we have seen and heard" (Acts 4:20).

What happened? Why this dramatic transformation from cowardice to courage? What enabled Peter, as well as the rest of the apostles, to suddenly live with such boldness that, remembering the question of Jesus, "Will you lay down your life for My sake?" (John 13:38), they willingly met their own martyrs' deaths? Pentecost had come! And with it, God the Father had sent the same Spirit that raised Christ from the dead to take up residence in each of them with supernatural power. This same Spirit lives today in the lives of each and every believer.

As we journey through these pages, we will meet the Holy Spirit afresh and anew—the same Holy Spirit who lives in every believer and longs to fill us with divine power and produce the fruit of His own life through us. Every word in every sentence of this volume is written with the prayer to move and motivate you to begin a great adventure in a whole new dimension of Christian living, empowered and led by this very same Holy Spirit who dramatically transformed the disciples two thousand years ago.

Along this journey we might find that some of us are a bit like those men and women Paul encountered at Ephesus who exclaimed, "We have not so much as heard whether there is a Holy Spirit" (Acts 19:2). If this is you, I am about to introduce you to the most important person you will ever meet. We will move on to see what the Holy Spirit *in you* entails. One of life's greatest discoveries is to awaken to the fact that the Lord really is alive and living in you in the person of the Holy Spirit. The apostle Paul is still asking believers, "Do you not know that you are the temple of God and that the Spirit of God dwells in you?" (1 Corinthians 3:16).

Continuing the journey, we will observe the Holy Spirit *upon you*. We can experience the same thing the early believers experienced. The Bible records, "You shall receive power when the Holy Spirit has come upon you" (Acts 1:8). The Holy Spirit who lives in you also comes upon you with anointing power for certain tasks in life.

> One of life's greatest discoveries is to awaken to the fact that the Lord really is alive and living in you in the person of the Holy Spirit.

This truth will be accompanied by the reality of the Holy Spirit living *through you*. The secret of victorious Christian living is allowing the Spirit who resides in us

3

to live His life through us. Jesus said, "'He who believes in Me, as the Scripture has said, out of his heart will flow rivers of living water.' But this He spoke concerning the [Holy] Spirit" (John 7:38–39).

Not only does He long to live through us, but we are about to discover what it means that the Holy Spirit is *for you*. He is your Advocate. The Bible informs us that "having believed, you were sealed with the Holy Spirit of promise, who is the guarantee of our inheritance" (Ephesians 1:13–14).

However, there is another side to the coin. It comes with a warning. Did you know that the Holy Spirit can be *against you*? Isaiah warned of those who "rebelled and grieved His Holy Spirit; so He turned Himself against them" (Isaiah 63:10). In the New Testament Jesus gave a stern warning saying, "Every sin and blasphemy will be forgiven . . . , but the blasphemy against the Spirit will not be forgiven" (Matthew 12:31). As the pages unfold before us, we will discover the true meaning of Jesus' words in this sobering passage.

Finally, we will close with a reminder that the Holy Spirit is *with us* always. We can hold to the precious promise that He will abide with us forever. The night before the crucifixion, Jesus left us with these words:

I will pray the Father, and He will give you another Helper, that He may abide with you forever—the Spirit of truth, whom the world cannot receive, because it neither sees Him nor knows Him; but you know Him, for He dwells with you and will be in you. (John 14:16–17)

So let's begin the journey to see how, in reality, it is God Himself in the person of the Holy Spirit who is with you, in you, and for you, and who longs to live through you.

1   MEET THE HOLY SPIRIT

*A*llow me the privilege of introducing you to the Holy Spirit. Perhaps there has never been another person as misrepresented and misunderstood as He. He is not some mysterious, nebulous force that can be equated to the famous *Star Wars* saying, "May the Force be with you." Nor, for those who know something of the Bible, did He show up on the scene for the first time on the day of Pentecost in an upper room on Mount Zion in the city of Jerusalem.

Let's begin with a foundational statement: The Holy Spirit is God. One of the foundational truths of orthodox Christianity is the belief that God is one and yet He eternally exists in three persons: Father, Son, and Holy Spirit. In theological jargon this is called the Trinity, three in one, and it is a great mystery. It has been revealed to us in various ways through the Bible but can be challenging to wrap our minds around. I have come to the conclusion that if I could understand all there is to know about the Godhead in my own limited mind, there would not be much to it. It is simply a theological truth that manifests itself from the first chapter of Genesis to the end of the book of Revelation, and because it is rooted in sacred Scripture, must be taken by faith. Many have attempted to explain the reality of the Trinity through metaphors and analogies, but none of them are completely valid.

> We cannot separate the Godhead. The Father, the Son, and the Holy Spirit are one . . . three in one. They always have been, and They always will be.

Some believe that the Father is the God of the Old Testament, the Son, Jesus Christ, is the God of the Gospels, and the Holy Spirit is the God of the book of Acts and the rest of the New Testament. But this is heretical thinking. Jesus did not just show up in the manger at Bethlehem. He was from the beginning. Neither did the Holy Spirit just show up at Pentecost. He was there from the beginning. We cannot separate the Godhead. The Father, the Son, and the Holy Spirit are one . . . three in one. They always have been, and they always will be.

There are 31,102 verses in the Bible, and the Holy Spirit shows up in the first two: "In the beginning God created the heavens and the earth. The earth was without form, and void; and darkness was on the face of the deep. And the Spirit of God was hovering over the face of the waters" (Genesis 1:1–2). He was there way back in the beginning at creation, "hovering over the face of the waters." In fact, there has never been a time when the Holy Spirit was not here manifesting the mighty presence and power of God.

The Father, the Son, and the Holy Spirit all were active in creation. It is said of the Father that "in the beginning God created the heavens and the earth" (Genesis 1:1). It is said of the Son that "In the beginning was the Word. . . . All things were made through Him, and without Him nothing was made that was made" (John 1:1, 3). So that we might never be confused as to the identity of this "Word," John went on to add, "The Word became flesh and dwelt among us, and we beheld His glory, the glory as of the only begotten of the Father, full of grace and truth" (John 1:14). Further, as mentioned above, the Holy Spirit, being a member of this triune God, was there as well, doing His part in the creation event.

Repeated in every Jewish synagogue all over the world in every Sabbath service is the Shema, the Jewish confession of faith: "Hear, O Israel: the LORD our God, the LORD is one!" (Deuteronomy 6:4). This confession is immediately followed by what Jesus referred to in the New Testament as the greatest commandment, "You shall love the LORD your God with all your heart, with all your soul, and with all your strength" (Deuteronomy 6:5). As followers of Christ, our Messiah, we affirm this truth—the Lord is one! Yet Scripture is clear in revealing that this one God is manifested to us in three persons: the Father, the Son, and the Holy Spirit. The apostle Paul made this crystal clear in his benediction to the church in Corinth: "The grace of the Lord Jesus Christ, and the love of God, and the communion of the Holy Spirit be with you all" (2 Corinthians 13:14).

Jesus made this emphatic claim in dialogue with the Jews when He said bluntly, "I and My Father are one" (John 10:30). Earlier, at Jesus' baptism in the Jordan River, Matthew recorded, "When He had been baptized, Jesus came up immediately from the water; and behold, the heavens were opened to Him, and He saw the Spirit of God descending like a dove and alighting upon Him. And suddenly a voice came from heaven, saying, 'This is My beloved Son, in whom I am well pleased'" (Matthew 3:16–17). As Jesus, the Son, stood in the waters of baptism, the Father spoke from heaven, and the Spirit descended like a dove.

Then as Jesus was about to physically leave us and just

before He ascended, He left us with a Great Commission: "Go therefore and make disciples . . . baptizing them in the name of the Father and of the Son and of the Holy Spirit" (Matthew 28:19). Thus, we join our Jewish friends in confessing the Shema, "The LORD our God, the LORD is one!" But we understand that this God is the great Three in One, manifesting Himself to us in all His glory as the Father, the Son, and the Holy Spirit.

We will discover in these pages that the Holy Spirit has always been at work in our lives. It is He who convicts us, converts us, commends us, commands us, consoles us, and comforts us. It is He who ultimately completes us. We will get to know the Holy Spirit who knows everything there is to know about us. He is an essential part of our journey toward finding the fullness of joy in life.

2 GETTING TO KNOW HIM

*T*he apostle Paul, upon arriving in Ephesus, inquired of some early believers regarding their knowledge of the Holy Spirit and was met with this reply: "We have not so much as heard whether there is a Holy Spirit" (Acts 19:2). Sadly, the same response could be said of many believers who have been sitting in their local churches for years. The emphasis on who the Holy Spirit is and what He does is severely lacking in many pulpits, so much so that He often becomes the forgotten member of the Godhead.

As we have previously discussed, the Holy Spirit is God Himself. He is an invisible yet inseparable member of the triune God—the Father, the Son, and the Holy Spirit. Much is often made of the Father and the Son and not enough of the Spirit. The Holy Spirit is God who comes to indwell us with the promise never to leave us and to empower us for Christian service. He is at work in our conversion. He convicts us of our sin and draws us to Christ. He seals our faith and gives us the power to live the Christian life.

Living the Christian life is not difficult—it is impossible without the person and power of God's Spirit residing in us. If you have placed your trust in Christ for salvation, then the Holy Spirit has come to take up residency in your life. He is alive in you at this very moment. It is time to get to know Him.

> Much is often made of the Father and the Son and not enough of the Spirit. The Holy Spirit is God who comes to indwell us with the promise never to leave us and to empower us for Christian service.

Speaking of the salvation experience, each person in this Trinity plays a vital role in your decision of coming to Christ. The Father is the *source* of salvation. It all stems from Him. From the moment Adam and Eve ate the forbidden fruit, God's plan of salvation kicked into gear. He killed an innocent animal and with its skins covered their sin. This first taste of blood atonement can be traced down through the pages of Scripture until it ultimately culminates on a Roman cross outside the city gates of Jerusalem.

If the Father is the source of our salvation, then its *course* is found in the Son, the Lord Jesus. The road to eternal life must come through Him. He made this truth crystal clear when He said, "I am the way, the truth, and the life. No one comes to the Father except through Me"

(John 14:6). The Father is the source, and the Son is the course of our salvation. And the Holy Spirit? He is the *force* behind it all.

When delivering His final instructions to the disciples before His departure back to heaven, Jesus said, "If I depart, I will send Him [the Holy Spirit] to you. And when He has come, He will convict the world of sin, and . . . He will guide you into all truth" (John 16:7–8, 13). To *convict* means to bring to light. It is the Holy Spirit who flips on the light to expose the hidden nature of our sin. Having thus convicted us of our sin, the Holy Spirit then does His work of drawing us to Christ, guiding us into all truth, and performing the work of regeneration in us. The Bible declares we are "born again . . . of the Spirit" (John 3:7, 8). With God the Father as the source, God the Son as the course, and God the Holy Spirit as the force, when we get to heaven, we might just discover we had a lot less to do with getting there on our own than we might have thought.

> When we get to heaven, we might just discover we had a lot less to do with getting there on our own than we might have thought.

One of the most liberating discoveries in the life of every believer is an awakening to the importance of the personality and deity of the Holy Spirit. If, in fact, He lives in you, it stands to reason that you would like to get to know Him in the intimacy of a close and abiding personal relationship. Dorothy in *The Wizard of Oz* said it best: "There's no place like home." And "home" for the Holy Spirit is in your heart. This is where He gets comfortable and resides. It is past time for some of us to make Him welcome and get to know Him.

Some are on a quest to "get more" of the Holy Spirit. But remember, He is a person and not some mystical force or substance that can be measured on a human scale. If we know Christ as a personal Savior, then we have all of the Holy Spirit abiding in us that we will ever need. If we begin to think of Him in terms of some external substance that might enable us or empower us with various supernatural abilities, then our quest will lead us on a journey to seek more of Him—but that road leads only to a cul-de-sac or, in some cases, even a dead end.

However, when we begin to think of the Holy Spirit as a person and not just some mystical power, then the focus of our search will no longer be a quest to "get more of Him." Rather, we will become consumed with how to give Him more of us. He is a person. He is living in us. And He wants more of us; He wants every room in our hearts.

We all have several rooms in our hearts—a family room, an office room, a playroom, and so forth. Christ's desire today is to become Lord over every room in our hearts as we surrender to the Holy Spirit.

The secret to victorious Christian living is not getting more of the Holy Spirit but giving Him more of you. Get to know Him. After all, He has chosen to live in you.

3 SIGNED, SEALED, AND DELIVERED

*R*ecently the front page of our local newspaper carried the story of a raid on a large counterfeit enterprise that was operating in a local warehouse district. Fake Gucci, Chanel, and Louis Vuitton merchandise with a street value of over forty million dollars was confiscated, and the operators of the criminal enterprise were arrested. A simple ten-dollar sweatshirt, when labeled with a fake Chanel logo, could have generated a bonanza of well over a thousand dollars on the street. There are a lot of counterfeit operations taking place today. On a recent visit to New York, it seemed impossible to walk a block without seeing people selling fake designer handbags and watches.

Sadly, counterfeit Christianity is also a reality. Thus, the question arises, "How can we know that our faith is real or if it is, in fact, fake?" Authentic believers have a seal, a stamp of authority that identifies them to an increasingly wondering and woke world. Paul described this mark of authenticity by saying, "In Him you also trusted, after you heard the word of truth, the gospel of your salvation; in whom also, having believed, you were sealed with the Holy Spirit of promise, who is the guarantee of our inheritance until the redemption of the purchased possession, to the praise of His glory" (Ephesians 1:13–14). Did you know that when you believed in Christ and transferred your trust to Him alone for your salvation, God put His seal, His stamp of approval on you? "You were sealed with the Holy Spirit."

> Did you know that when you believed in Christ and transferred your trust to Him alone for your salvation, God put His seal, His stamp of approval on you?

When Paul stated that "you were sealed with the Holy Spirit," he wrote these words in a verb tense that indicates the event occurred at a distinct and definite moment in time past, and that you had nothing to do with it. In the Greek syntax of this verse, the subject doesn't act, it is acted upon by someone outside. Paul was speaking here of something that is more like a snapshot from the past and not a video. It is a done deal. When you came to know Jesus as your personal Savior, God put a seal on you that Paul called the "Holy Spirit of promise." And God keeps His promises.

A seal speaks of three things—authenticity, ownership, and security. Interestingly, John the Baptist used the same Greek term for "seal" when, speaking of Jesus of Nazareth, he declared, "He who has received His testimony has certified that God is true" (John 3:33). The "seal" Paul talked about in Ephesians 1 reveals that we are real, authentic believers.

When you were saved, God certified you and stamped you with the Holy Spirit—His seal of approval to show that you are the real thing. Most of us have heard of the "Good Housekeeping Seal of Approval." In 1909, *Good Housekeeping* magazine introduced its seal of approval. The seal was (and still is) awarded to products that have passed rigorous standards set by *Good Housekeeping*, allowing the company to confidently suggest dependable products to consumers across all these decades.

In the context of the Roman world in which Paul lived, letters were sealed with hot wax and then stamped with a seal from a unique signet ring to show the authenticity of the author. Most of us today have had the experience of going to a notary public to certify an agreement with another party. After signing the document, the notary embosses the contract with a seal to show authenticity. In a similar fashion God has "sealed" you with His own Spirit to authenticate your faith and give you the confidence that the transaction of salvation you made with God the Father through His Son, the Lord Jesus Christ, is real.

Think back to the day you came to know Christ in the free pardoning of sin, the day you were, in His words, "born again." The Holy Spirit was there. At that moment God put His Holy Spirit in you to certify the authenticity of your faith. When we sometimes wonder if it is all really real, if we are authentic believers, we need only look for the seal—"The Spirit Himself bears witness with our spirit that we are children of God" (Romans 8:16). A seal speaks of authenticity, that something is really real.

> When we sometimes wonder if it is all really real, if we are authentic believers, we need only look for the seal.

A seal also is the indicator of ownership—proof that we actually belong to someone else. Paul explained in 2 Corinthians 1:22 that God has "sealed us and given us the Spirit in our hearts as a guarantee." The NIV translates this verse as God having "set His seal of ownership on us." When God stamped us with His seal of approval, the Holy Spirit, He was reminding us that we belong to Him.

When I was a little boy, my uncle owned a ranch in Texas outside the little mountain hamlet of Camp Wood.

I always loved being there when it was time to brand the new calves. While one worker held the calf down, another would take a hot iron branding tool and sear my uncle's initials into the animal's hindquarters. This mark would be there for the rest of the cow's life to indicate who owned it. It was not unusual for cattle to occasionally get through a fence and wander onto someone else's property. The brand was there as indisputable evidence of the ownership of the cows.

This is the same principle Paul was speaking of when he said, "You were sealed with the Holy Spirit of promise." God put His brand on you. You belong to Him, now and forever. This is God's way of indicating that when we place our trust in Him, He places the Holy Spirit in our hearts to seal the fact that we belong to Him. The Holy Spirit is our seal to authenticate our salvation and to let the world know that we belong to Christ.

But there is more. God seals us with the Holy Spirit to let us know that we are secure. Ironically, we find the same Greek word Paul used to indicate our authenticity and ownership as believers also used in Matthew 27:66, in the account of the burial of Christ. Once Jesus was in His burial place, Scripture says the tomb was sealed with a Roman seal, and a guard was set to watch over it. A sealing of string and wax was affixed to the tomb to protect it from tampering or theft. The seal of the Holy Spirit not only speaks of authenticity and ownership but also gives us confidence that we are secure in Him. What a comforting revelation to know that we are sealed by the Holy Spirit and secure in Him from anything that might come our way.

> What a comforting revelation to know that we are sealed by the Holy Spirit and secure in Him from anything that might come our way.

If you are "in Christ," God has sealed you with His Holy Spirit. You are for real. He has placed His stamp of ownership and authenticity on you. You are secure against any effort of Satan to break that seal. Let's pause for a moment and meditate on these amazing words: "In Him you also trusted, after you heard the word of truth, the gospel of your salvation; in whom also, having believed, you were sealed with the Holy Spirit of promise, who is the guarantee of our inheritance until the redemption of the purchased possession, to the praise of His glory" (Ephesians 1:13–14).

You are signed and sealed by the Holy Spirit, and one day at His coming you will be delivered to the Father—His own purchased possession. The next time you observe a notary's seal proving a document's authenticity, let it be a reminder of the seal of the Holy Spirit that God has placed on your own heart.

4 A GOOD-FAITH DEPOSIT

*T*here are many aspects involved in our relationship with the Holy Spirit. The Bible informs us that He is not simply our "seal" but our "deposit"—our *guarantee* that in the end, God will be found true to His word and all will be made right. Paul said, "You were sealed with the Holy Spirit of promise, who is the guarantee of our inheritance until the redemption of the purchased possession, to the praise of His glory" (Ephesians 1:13–14). The Greek word Paul chose that we translate as *guarantee* means that a deposit has been made that indicates the full amount will later be paid in the same kind of payment as the deposit. It is a down payment, an installment, a smaller part of the full price to be received at a later time. The Holy Spirit is your guarantee from God the Father, His deposit in your life, until He returns to receive us all unto Himself.

My first job as a high school student was in the stockroom of a small independent shoe store on the east side of Fort Worth. After proving myself for several weeks, I was promoted to the sales floor, where I interacted with customers in an attempt to sell them a pair of shoes. Money was tight on our side of town, and it was not unusual for those who had little means to make a deposit on a pair of shoes. We would then hold those shoes in a special section of the stockroom until the customer's next pay period, when they would return to complete the purchase and take their new shoes home. I learned that when someone made a deposit on a pair of shoes, it was a guarantee—a sure thing—that they would be back with their final payment to pick them up. When a customer made a deposit like that, we knew they would be back. We would see them again because they would not forfeit their investment.

In the same way, the Holy Spirit is God's own deposit in each of our hearts. This deposit assures us of two things. First, that our final purchase is guaranteed. And second, the One who bought us, the Lord Jesus, is coming back to close the deal. In Paul's words, the Holy Spirit is our "guarantee."

Anyone who has ever purchased a home knows the meaning of this term. The real estate agent calls it "earnest money." It is the deposit you make when you finalize the real estate deal and sign the contract. Your deposit shows you mean business. It is your promise that full payment will come at the time of closing on the property. Should you fail to close at the proper time, you lose your deposit. It is your guarantee that you mean business.

When you were saved, what happened? God put the Holy Spirit in your heart. He is God's deposit in you that guarantees the final purchase. Since God always keeps His promises, you will never lose this deposit.

This is the difference between the activity of the Holy Spirit in the Old Testament and the New Testament. Before the cross, in the old dispensation, the Holy Spirit would come upon believers, but when they became unfaithful, He would depart from them. One of the saddest verses in all the Bible says of Samson that "the LORD [Holy Spirit] had departed from him" (Judges 16:20). In David's heartfelt prayer of remorse and repentance after living in adultery with Bathsheba, he pled with God, saying, "Do not take Your Holy Spirit from me" (Psalm 51:11). On this side of Calvary, however, after Christ's sacrifice for sin on the cross, the Holy Spirit comes to indwell believers and never leave them again. He is our deposit from God the Father that guarantees Christ's final possession of us.

> The Holy Spirit is God's deposit in you guaranteeing the final purchase. And He always keeps His promises.

This is the very thing Jesus promised in the upper room the night before the crucifixion. "I will pray the Father, and He will give you another Helper, that He may abide with you forever" (John 14:16). And so that we might never wonder as to the identity of this other "Helper," Jesus affirmed in verse 17 that He is "the Spirit of truth." Paul added that He is the "guarantee of our inheritance" (Ephesians 1:14). God's Holy Spirit in you is God's deposit guaranteeing you eternal life. The Holy Spirit in our hearts brings peace and joy and guarantees that there is more to come. The best is yet to be.

When God placed the Holy Spirit within you, it was His guarantee that He is coming back. Paul said it is "until the redemption of the purchased possession, to the praise of His glory" (Ephesians 1:14). Our "blessed hope" (Titus 2:13) is the fact that Jesus Christ is coming again. We have been purchased by the blood of Christ for His own possession. He has deposited the Holy Spirit in our hearts to assure us that our salvation is secure and that one day He will come again to finish what He started. On God's calendar of eternity, there is a date already fixed when Jesus Christ will come again to close the deal with us. Meanwhile, we are living in that great "until He comes."

The Bible says, "If the Spirit of Him who raised Jesus

> The Holy Spirit within us is just a foretaste, a portent, a harbinger of all the glory that is to come.

from the dead dwells in you, He who raised Christ from the dead will also give life to your mortal bodies through His Spirit who dwells in you" (Romans 8:11). Until then, the Holy Spirit is our deposit guaranteeing the One who bought us with His own blood is coming again to take us home with Him. The Holy Spirit within us is just a foretaste, a portent, a harbinger of all the glory that is to come.

The next time you make a deposit into your bank account, let it remind you of both the deposit God has placed in your heart and the promise that eternal life is guaranteed to any and all who place their trust in Him. The Lord has sent His Spirit to live in you, to put His seal on you, and as a deposit in your heart to give you the assurance that the very one who bought you with the price of His own blood is coming back to take you home with Him.

5 THE HOLY SPIRIT AND YOUR BIBLE

*I*f you have ever opened the pages of the Bible and read a few verses, you have encountered the Holy Spirit, whether you were conscious of it or not. The authorship of the first five books of the Bible is attributed to Moses, but in a very real sense, Moses did not write the Pentateuch. Nor did John actually write the gospel that bears his name. Nor was Paul actually the author of the many New Testament epistles that bear his name. "Holy men of God spoke as they were moved by the Holy Spirit" (2 Peter 1:21). Your Bible—every verse, every word, every syllable of it—was authored by the Holy Spirit.

Almost all the books written in centuries past have been lost in the darkness of antiquity. But the Bible is different from any book ever penned by any person. Actually, it is a library of sixty-six different books written over a span of more than fourteen hundred years by at least forty different authors. And what a group they were. Some were kings, others were prophets, rabbis, doctors, shepherds, and even rough, callus-handed fishermen. Yet woven through every page of the Bible are the threads of one single theme of redemption and one theology. There is no explanation for its unique and lasting nature other than the statement that behind the pen of each writer was the hand of the Holy Spirit Himself.

We read that as these authors were speaking and writing, "they were moved by the Holy Spirit" (2 Peter 1:21). But how did that happen? Luke gave us a bit of insight on this when he wrote of Paul's shipwreck off the coast of Crete. In describing the shipwreck, Luke chose the same Greek word translated in 2 Peter 1:21 as *moved* to describe how the sailors were driven by the winds. In the midst of a fierce storm, the sailors on board lost all control, unable to steer or guide the vessel because of the strong winds. They stayed on their posts, busy at their tasks, but they could no longer guide the ship because of the powerful gale-force winds they faced. The winds took over and took the ship wherever they blew. In the sailors' words, "We let her drive" (Acts 27:15). Though the sailors on board the ship were active in seeking to secure the mast and hold the rudder, they had no control over where the ship was driven by the winds.

So it was with the Bible writers. They were active with pen in hand. Their personalities and writing styles are certainly unique in Scripture. But, like the wind, they had no control over where the Holy Spirit was leading them. The writings were not

Behind every word you read in your daily Bible devotions, you can see the Holy Spirit at work.

their own. They were the words of God. The Holy Spirit guided them. God made this plain to Jeremiah when He said, "I have put My words in your mouth" (Jeremiah 1:9). Behind every word you read in your daily Bible devotions, you can see the Holy Spirit at work. And not only does He give you those words, but He illumines them for you as He guides you "into all truth" (John 16:13).

Your Bible has a supernatural origin. Writing to his young understudy, Timothy, Paul insisted that "all Scripture is given by inspiration of God" (2 Timothy 3:16). That little three-letter word *all* is fully inclusive. The psalmist David said "the law of the LORD is perfect" (Psalm 19:7). Later, his son Solomon added that "every word of God is pure" (Proverbs 30:5). At the very beginning of Jesus' public ministry, when He burst forth from the obscurity of the carpenter's shop and was tempted by the devil in the wilderness, He replied with Scripture, saying, "It is written, 'Man shall not live by bread alone, but by every word that proceeds from the mouth of God'" (Matthew 4:4). Yes, every word of Scripture is pure and has proceeded straight from the mouth of God Himself.

Reading 2 Timothy 3:16 again, we see that "all Scripture is given by inspiration of God." It is *given*. That is, it is supernatural. It originated with God and not with humankind. Your Bible is God's gift to you. It is given to you "by inspiration of God." This phrase literally means "God breathed." These are God's words, delivered to us through men who wrote as they were inspired by the Spirit. God used men in the process, but He did not just breathe *on* them. He breathed *out of them* the Word of God. Just as a skilled musical composer creates a score using a flute, a trumpet, and an assortment of other brass, percussion, and woodwind instruments, so God chose His own specific instruments through whom He would give us His infallible Word. Each of these Bible writers was as uniquely different as flutes and trumpets are. Yet God chose them, and the Holy Spirit breathed

> Just as a skilled musical composer creates a score using a flute, a trumpet, and an assortment of other . . . instruments, so God chose His own specific instruments through whom He would give us His infallible Word.

out the words of God through them and onto the printed page for all posterity, a beautiful symphony of God's own words to us coming together in perfect harmony.

The Bible comes under great scrutiny by those who are skeptical of scriptural truth, but one thing is certain. When we view the Bible, it is not on trial—we are. God's Word has withstood the test of time, and it will still be the Book of all books when all the writings of mortals have vanished into obscurity. It is no wonder David declared, "Your word I have hidden in my heart, that I might not sin against You" (Psalm 119:11).

The best way to get to know the Holy Spirit is to let Him speak to you each morning through the words of Scripture He authored so long ago. Hide them in your heart, so you won't sin against Him.

6 A NEW BEGINNING

My father's family moved to Texas from Tennessee back in the 1800s. When I was a boy, we would make our annual summer road trip back to the Volunteer State to visit, among others, my great-aunt Ann. I loved those long car trips in the days before interstate highways. I can still remember the excitement I felt when we passed a barn that had "Visit Rock City" painted on its roof or the fun of reading the old Burma Shave signs along the way. We'd stay in her house, and I slept on an iron bed with a feather mattress. I once heard an old preacher say life was like those old feather mattresses. I can relate to that—anyone who has ever slept on one of those supersoft beds has awakened in a ball in the middle of the mattress. The bed was firm on both iron ends but, oh, that sagging middle.

Some Christians live their entire lives like that. They are firm on both ends. On the front end, they can point to a specific moment in time when they placed their trust in Christ, and they live with the assurance that they are born again. They are also firm on the other end: they know they are going to heaven when they die. But between those two events, they live their lives like a feather mattress, often sagging and without strength and joy in their Christian walk.

Luke opened the book of Acts with these words: "The former account I made . . . of all that Jesus began both to do and teach" (Acts 1:1). Wait. Did you catch that? The Gospels are only the account of what Jesus *began* to do. He is not finished. He was just getting started. He is still active. He may not physically be here today, but He continues to use the Holy Spirit—and you—to accomplish His work.

> The Gospels are only the account of what Jesus *began* to do. He is not finished. He was just getting started.

We often call the book of Acts the "Acts of the Apostles." But that's not really what it is. It is about the acts of the Holy Spirit, which are still being accomplished today in and through you and me. Luke's gospel tells us what Jesus did and taught in His physical body. The book of Acts tells us what the Holy Spirit continues to do in and through His spiritual body, the church. What an encouragement to know that Jesus is still at work and using the partnership between you and the Holy Spirit to present to the world a picture of Himself today.

Acts is the story of what the Lord Jesus continues to do through the work of the Holy Spirit in our lives. You will notice, however, that the book of Acts ends rather abruptly. It just stops. That is because the story goes on and on, all the way to today.

> God is not interested in us doing something *for* Him. The secret to victorious Christian living is allowing the Holy Spirit to live and do something *through* us.

Anyone who has sought to live the Christian life has come to the discovery that it is not difficult—no, it is, in fact, impossible! Impossible, that is, if we seek to live it in our own strength. God is not interested in us doing something *for* Him. The secret to victorious Christian living is allowing the Holy Spirit to live and do something *through* us. It is no wonder Paul exclaimed, "Christ in you, the hope of glory" (Colossians 1:27).

When you awaken to the Holy Spirit's power in you, a new dimension of Christian living will greet you. This is what Jesus was getting at when He said, "Most assuredly, I say to you, he who believes in Me, the works that I do he will do also; and greater works than these he will do, because I go to My Father" (John 14:12). This is an amazing statement. Jesus is saying we will not just *equal* what He did while on earth but we will *exceed* His works. Some people see this verse, roll up their sleeves, and go out seeking to work harder and harder in their attempt to do something for God. And they meet with failure every time.

The key to understanding Jesus' meaning here is found in His statement that He was returning to the Father. We find the answer four verses later: "I will pray the Father, and He will give you another Helper, that He may abide with you forever" (John 14:16). In that upper room conversation, Jesus went on to promise, "I will not leave you orphans; I will come to you" (John 14:18). And come back He did, in the power and presence of the Holy Spirit who accomplishes greater works in us, never leaves us, and empowers us to live the Christian life.

After Jesus left the disciples bodily, they gathered in the upper room and waited "for the Promise of the Father" (Acts 1:4)—the coming of the Holy Spirit. They didn't gather there until they were worthy to receive Him. Who of us is worthy in our own power? They waited for the Helper that Jesus had promised, "the Holy Spirit, whom the Father will send in My name, He will teach you all things, and bring to your remembrance all things that I said to you" (John 14:26). True to His word, the Holy Spirit fell upon all of them on the day of Pentecost and they—and we—have never been the same since.

The power of Jesus does not end with the gospel records. He had just begun. The Holy Spirit continues His work today on this earth in you, through you, for you, and upon you. Victorious life is about the Holy Spirit *and* you. Now it is time to turn the page and discover all that having the Holy Spirit *in you* means.

7 A EUREKA MOMENT

ureka is one of those words that has muscled and maneuvered its way into our modern English vernacular. Most of us have had a "eureka moment," a "wow" moment, a snapshot in time when a sudden inspiration or insight opened our eyes to a previously unknown truth or reality. Eureka moments always come with an exclamation mark attached. They happen when a student, after struggling for a time with a math problem, suddenly sees the answer to the equation. "Eureka! Wow!" They happen when we discover that the person we have been dating has become the one we cannot live the rest of our lives without. Put another exclamation mark there. Eureka!

But did you know the word *eureka* is a New Testament word? It is found in John 1:41. The word escaped the lips of Andrew, who, after coming to follow Jesus of Nazareth, immediately sought out his brother, Simon Peter, and excitedly exclaimed, "We have found [eureka!] the Messiah." After all the prophets pointing to this event, after centuries

> Awakening to the fact that the Holy Spirit is *in you* can become your own eureka moment.

of waiting on the promise of a coming Redeemer, "Eureka! He is here! And what is more, we have found Him!" They had found Him all right, and as they lived with Him for the next three years, their lives were repeatedly filled with these eureka moments. Awakening to the fact that the Holy Spirit is *in you* can become your own eureka moment.

Anyone who has stood on the Mount of Olives or seen pictures of the Holy City of Jerusalem has seen the golden dome of the Mosque of Omar prominently situated on a high plateau within the eastern gate of the old city walls. Long before a mosque occupied that holy terrain, there stood another building unmatched in its grandeur and splendor. The Jewish temple, built by King Solomon in 957 BCE, once stood on or very near the same spot. Adorned with its bronze pillars and overlayed in pure gold, it glistened each morning as the sun rose over the eastern mountain range of the city. It was the center of Jewish worship, and within its hallowed confines, behind a thick veil, resided the holy ark of the covenant. Once a year, on the high holy Day of Atonement, Yom Kippur, the high priest alone would enter into the holy of holies beyond the veil and sprinkle the blood of the sacrifice over the mercy seat of the ark in order to make atonement for the sins of the people. Then the shekinah glory of God would fill the sacred room as God would visit within this Holy Place.

Two completely different Greek words appear often in our New Testament, and both are translated into the English word *temple*. Discovering the difference between the two brings a eureka moment to our own experience. The Greek word *hieron* describes the entire temple complex consisting of the Holy Place, the court of the women, the court of the Gentiles, Solomon's portico, and all that stood on the temple mount. We find this word in Mark 13:3, describing Jesus sitting on the Mount of Olives "opposite the temple." His view consisted of the entire temple area. The word also appears in Mark 11:15 when Jesus was on the temple mount, turning over the tables of the money changers who sold their wares "in the temple." These hawkers were not inside the Holy Place or the actual edifice, yet they were still on the temple mount. This word *hieron* refers to the entire temple area.

However, we find another word translated as *temple* in our New Testament as well. This word is used to describe the holy of holies, that sacred place within the Holy Place behind the veil where God Himself came to meet with His people. This word appears in Matthew 27:51 and Mark 15:38, describing how the veil in the temple was torn in two from top to bottom. In contrast to the previous word, this word describes only the area of the holy of holies in the temple.

Are you ready for an awesome thought, a eureka moment? When Paul asked, "Do you not know that your body is the temple of the Holy Spirit who is in you, whom you have from God, and you are not your own" (1 Corinthians 6:19), he used this second word for "temple." In other words, your heart is God's very own temple, His own holy of holies, and the Holy Spirit is *in you*!

> Your heart is God's very own temple, His own holy of holies, and the Holy Spirit is *in you*!

When you came to know Christ and trusted in Him for your eternal salvation, a miracle took place in your heart. The Holy Spirit took your very spirit that was dead and made it alive. At that moment He came to live *in you*. You became His dwelling place, the place where He meets you in worship.

As we read the Old Testament, we discover that God had a temple for His people. They journeyed to the temple from long distances to celebrate their feasts, to present their sacrifices, and to worship Him with psalms of praise. But now, in this new dispensation of grace, God exchanged the two concepts. Instead of a temple for His people, now He has a people for His temple. No longer is the experience of His presence limited to one man, the high priest, on one specific day per year. Instead, God has chosen to take up residency in you and in every other believer—not just for one day but for all time.

Yes, the reality is that "you are not your own. . . . You were bought at a price" (1 Corinthians 6:19–20). It is of little wonder that Paul concluded this verse with a challenge for each of us: "Therefore glorify God in your body and in your spirit, which are God's."

As you read these words, let me remind you how indescribably valuable you are to God, so valuable that He has chosen to take up residency within you. When you awaken to this amazing reality, you will find your very own eureka moment. The Holy Spirit is *in you*!

8 THE BAPTISM OF THE HOLY SPIRIT

I was not a follower of Christ very long before a well-meaning friend asked if I had been "baptized in the Holy Spirit." Being on fire for Christ, I wanted all that God had for me, so I began to search the Scriptures to see what I might be missing. My friend believed that this was a second work of grace after conversion, leading to a deeper life. Others said it was simply the second half of the first work of grace in my life. But what does the Bible really mean when it says, "By one Spirit we were all baptized into one body" (1 Corinthians 12:13)?

From my search I became convinced that the Holy Spirit is the baptizer who, upon our conversion to the faith, baptizes us and immerses us into the body of Christ. For thirty-three years the world looked upon the physical body of Jesus. With His feet He walked among us, sometimes among great crowds and sometimes to meet individuals in solitude. From His lips escaped the most tender yet penetrating words ever spoken. With His piercing eyes He looked straight into each person's heart. With His ears He listened intently to pleas for mercy and help. With His hands He touched people individually at the point of their greatest need.

Today, He is no longer physically here. He no longer walks the shores of Galilee or the dusty trails of Judea. He ascended back to the Father. Today, you and I and every other believer comprise the visible body of Christ. And we are being watched by a needy world still desperate for a listening ear or a gentle touch. The truth of Scripture is that the bap-

> Today, you and I and every other believer comprise the visible body of Christ. And we are being watched by a needy world still desperate for a listening ear or a gentle touch.

tism of the Holy Spirit that the disciples experienced on the day of Pentecost (Acts 2) was the initial experience when the Holy Spirit came to live *in* them, never to leave them, empowering them for supernatural service in the expansion of the kingdom on earth. But when do we as modern-day believers receive that baptism of the Holy Spirit?

Many sincere and deeply committed Christ followers see the baptism of the Holy Spirit as a second work of grace, subsequent to the salvation event and evidenced by speaking in an unknown tongue, the "tongues of men and of angels" (1 Corinthians 13:1). This view is often based on the interval of time that elapses in the book of Acts between conversion and baptism by the Spirit. Because the disciples received the Holy Spirit at a time well after they believed that Christ was Lord, today's adherents to the theory of a second work of grace believe that the baptism of the Holy Spirit is something to be sought. But the delay in Scripture was necessary because Jesus had not yet departed (John 7:39).

The group of believers who were gathered in the upper room that day experienced manifestations like the sound of a rushing, mighty wind; they saw tongues of fire resting on their heads; they spoke in a language that was miraculously understood by each hearer in their own language and dialect. The Holy Spirit came at that moment because at that point, Jesus had been glorified.

Peter later stood to preach on the temple mount and said, "Repent, and let every one of you be baptized in the name of Jesus Christ for the remission of sins; and you shall receive the gift of the Holy Spirit" (Acts 2:38). Peter made it plain. They no longer needed to wait for the Holy Spirit to come at a later time in a second work of grace.

They did not even need to ask for the Holy Spirit. What did they need to do? *Repent and be saved* was the only instruction. When they did, they would "receive the gift of the Holy Spirit." Right then, right there, at the moment of conversion.

While sincere believers today may differ on this point, we certainly all agree that the Holy Spirit has come to convict us of sin, to convince us of righteousness, to be the agent of regeneration, to indwell us, to seal us, to fill us, to empower us, and to lift up the Lord Jesus Christ through us to a lost world. Peripheral matters will get sorted out in heaven, when they will no longer matter.

This is the work of the Holy Spirit: to baptize us, to place us, to immerse us at conversion into the body of Christ just as Scripture says: "For by one Spirit we were all baptized into one body" (1 Corinthians 12:13). Note the use of the past tense in that statement. Nowhere in Scripture are we told that we *must be* baptized with the Holy Spirit. Why? Because the Bible is plain—if we are believers, we—all of us—*have been* baptized with the Holy Spirit already. Scripturally speaking in the

> Scripturally speaking in the New Testament, the baptism by the Holy Spirit always happens at the moment of conversion.

New Testament, the baptism by the Holy Spirit always happens at the moment of conversion. We never read in the Bible of a believer seeking the baptism of the Holy Spirit. There is no command anywhere in Scripture that we be baptized with the Holy Spirit. We will discover in a later chapter that there is, indeed, a command regarding the Holy Spirit. However, it is not to *be baptized by* Him but to *be filled with* Him.

Acts 2:4 states that on the day of Pentecost, "they were all filled with the Holy Spirit." Note Luke's use of the word *all* here. They were *all* baptized by the Holy Spirit. Scripture does not tell us that some were baptized in the Holy Spirit and some were not. Since that day every believer all over the world, in the moment they came to faith in Christ, "by one Spirit . . . were all baptized into one body"—the body of Christ (1 Corinthians 12:13).

Some say that Pentecost can be repeated. Why should it be? There is no need. It was a one-time event, in the same way that the incarnation of Jesus as a human baby in Bethlehem was a one-time event with no need of being repeated. Calvary, where Christ died for all our sins once and for all, was a one-time event; it will never need to be repeated. And so it was with Pentecost, the day the Spirit came to indwell each believer, never again to leave. At

Bethlehem we see *God with us.* At Calvary we see *God for us.* At Pentecost we see *God in us.* All three were one-time events with no need to be repeated.

For a believer to pray, "Lord, send the Holy Spirit like you did on the day of Pentecost," would be the same as praying, "Lord, send Jesus to Bethlehem to be born of a virgin." He already did! To pray, "Lord, send the Holy Spirit like you did on the day of Pentecost," would be the same as praying, "Lord, send Jesus to Calvary to die for our sins." He already did that. There is no more need for Pentecost to be repeated than there is for Bethlehem or Calvary to be repeated. As we will see in coming chapters, our desperate need is not the *baptism* of the Holy Spirit but the *filling* of the Holy Spirit and the discovery of His unique spiritual gifts with which He has endowed for the building up of the body of Christ.

The salvation experience is called a "conversion" because it is a transforming event. At the moment of conversion, the Holy Spirit baptizes the believer; He immerses us into the body of Christ. Our relationship with the Holy Spirit then is not so much a *second blessing* as it is a *growing experience*, in that the more of our lives we surrender to Him, the more He fills us with His presence. It becomes not just a second blessing but a third and a fourth and so on, throughout our entire Christian experience.

We should not get fixated on semantics at this point. My late friend Jack Taylor was fond of saying, "I would rather see someone who had the right thing and called it the wrong thing than to see someone who insisted he had the right thing and didn't have anything." At the moment of your conversion, the Holy Spirit immersed you into the body of Christ. Scripture calls this the baptism of the Holy Spirit: "By one Spirit we were all baptized into one body" (1 Corinthians 12:13).

9 THIRSTY? COME AND DRINK

*T*he Holy Spirit is *in* you right this very moment. But it is not so much for you to get a blessing as for you to become a blessing to others. Jesus said, "If anyone thirsts, let him come to Me and drink. He who believes in Me, as the Scripture has said, out of his heart will flow rivers of living water" (John 7:37–38). In the very next verse, so that no one could misunderstand His meaning, the Bible states, "But this He spoke concerning the Spirit" (John 7:39).

Jesus and His band of believers had journeyed from Galilee to Jerusalem with thousands of other pilgrims to celebrate the Feast of Tabernacles. It was a time of great joy as the people remembered God's deliverance of His people from the four-decades-long experience of wilderness wanderings. Booths were constructed all over the city as a reminder of their nomadic tent dwellings. For seven days the priests would trek down the hill to the pool of Siloam, fill their golden pitchers full of water, then ascend back to the temple mount and pour the water as a sacrifice over the altar. It was a vivid reminder of how God had provided water for the Israelites from the rock at Meribah to satisfy their desert thirst. People followed with trumpets of praise, singing, "With joy [we] will draw water from the wells of salvation" (Isaiah 12:3).

It was in the middle of this scene, "on the last day, that great day of the feast" (John 7:37), when Jesus spoke His famous words regarding living water. He observed how superficial the feast was in many ways. In a few days they would journey back to their homes to the same old heartaches and the same old way of life. Knowing nothing had changed in their hearts, Jesus stood up and cried with a very loud voice, "Come to Me and drink. . . . Out of [your] heart will flow rivers of living water." This was His way of telling them to stop enduring religion and start enjoying it.

> Jesus stood up and cried with a very loud voice, "Come to Me and drink. . . . Out of [your] heart will flow rivers of living water."

We are not much different today. Some think the answer to joy in life is education, but often their heads get bigger and their hearts emptier. Others seek activism and immerse themselves in work, work, work, staying busy even at doing good things. Others seek abstinence, thinking the more they give up, the more they please God. When we awaken to our personal eureka moment (the realization that the Holy Spirit is *in* us), that is when we stop enduring religion and begin to enjoy the relationship with Him.

In the midst of all the hallelujahs and hoopla of that day of the Feast of Tabernacles, Jesus began to cry out in a loud, emotional outburst. If we have ears to hear Him today, He is still saying to us, "If anyone thirsts, let him come to Me and drink. He who believes in Me, as the Scripture has said, out of his heart will flow rivers of living water."

Jesus began with an inquiry: "If anyone thirsts." His whole invitation is predicated on an "if." Have you ever been thirsty? How much would you pay for a bottle of water if you were really thirsty? Two dollars? Five dollars? If you found yourself in the desert about to die of thirst, how much would you pay for that same bottle of water? A truly thirsty person would pay almost any price.

The reason many believers are not enjoying the Spirit-filled life today is simple: they are not really thirsty for the things of God. The thirst Jesus referred to here was a spiritual thirst, not physical. Earlier He had said to a woman He met at a well, "Whoever drinks of the water that I shall give him will never thirst. But the water that I shall give him will become in him a fountain of water springing up into everlasting life" (John 4:14).

> We thirst for a lot of things in life, but do we have a thirst for Him? If we are not being filled, it is because we are not thirsty.

Jesus is still searching for the thirsty ones. People know if they are thirsty or not. If you have to ask if you are thirsty, you are not. We thirst for a lot of things in life, but do we have a thirst for Him? If we are not being filled, it is because we are not thirsty. Jesus makes an inquiry—*If anyone thirsts.* Anyone. This includes those who seem to have everything and those who have little. Anyone. *Everyone.* Even as I type this chapter, I wonder where the thirsty ones are who might be reading these words.

Our Lord continued in this passage with a word of invitation. "Come to Me." *Come.* This is one of the simplest words in the English language. A toddler learning to walk understands this word when she waddles shakily toward a parent whose arms are outstretched as they call, "Come to me." Jesus' arms are outstretched today with an invitation to come to Him, to do with our hearts what that little child does with her feet. "Come to Me."

Come to who? Jesus. The call is not to some devotional plan or some multistep formula. Just come to Jesus. Beware of plans or programs, principles or precepts. Begin by accepting His simple invitation: "Come to Me."

Next came an initiation. "Come to Me and drink." It is not enough to have a thirst. Thirst must be quenched by taking a drink. Jesus said when we drink from His cup of living water, we "will never thirst" again (John 4:14). All the water in the world is insufficient to quench your thirst if you do not drink it. Don't just look at the water or admire it. Drink it!

Finally in John 7, Jesus added, "He who believes in Me . . . out of his heart will flow rivers of living water." Faith is the victory. It doesn't *bring* the victory, it *is* the victory. And the result? Out of our innermost being will flow the living water of the Spirit so that we may be blessed in becoming a blessing to others.

As I have read and reread these words of Jesus, I have listened to Him crying out to us to come to Him and drink of this living water. The thing that most amazes me here, however, is that we should *need* such pleading from Him and that He should extend it to us. Shouldn't it be the other way around? Shouldn't we be doing the pleading, calling out to Him to let us come and drink? I wonder where the thirsty ones are today. Perhaps He is saying to someone reading these words right now, "Come to Me and drink."

The Holy Spirit is *in* you, but not just so you can get a blessing but that you might become a blessing as well—that out of your own innermost being will flow rivers of living water. Thirsty? Come to Jesus and drink.

10 YOU IN ME, AND I IN YOU

$\mathcal{T}$he evening before our Lord was brutally and brazenly nailed to a Roman cross outside the city gates of Jerusalem, He gathered His followers together for some final words. Looking into their troubled and confused eyes, He spoke these words to them: "A little while longer and the world will see Me no more, but you will see Me. Because I live, you will live also. At that day you will know that I am in My Father, and you in Me, and I in you" (John 14:19–20). With this amazing declaration, Jesus seeks to get us to fix our thoughts not on *who* we are or *what* we are or even *why* we are—but on *where* we are.

Think about this revelatory truth. Where is Jesus? He is in the Father. And where are you? According to Jesus, you are in Him! Look at you. You are in Christ, and He is in the Father. Talk about insulation. No matter what you are up against, no matter what comes your way today, you are in a good place. You are positioned in Christ, and He is in the Father. Nothing can possibly get to you that does

> No matter what you are up against . . . you are in a good place. You are positioned in Christ, and He is in the Father.

not first pass through God the Father and God the Son to reach you. And, if it penetrates that shield and gets that far, you can rest in the fact that there is a purpose for it in your life.

But that is not all. Jesus also said, "I am in you." Can you grasp it? Christ is taking care of the outside of you (you are in Me) and He is taking care of the inside of you (I am in you)! What better place to live your life?

As I write these words in my home study, we are experiencing another sweltering, blistering hot Texas summer day with the temperature once again over one hundred degrees. Thanks to the advent of air-conditioning, it is cool in my study. But there is something else that is essential in keeping our home cool in the summer and warm in the winter. Up in the attic, unseen from the rooms of our home, is a thick layer of foam insulation. It is a reminder to me that although I am not *isolated* from the world around me, I am *spiritually insulated* from it. And so are you if you have put your faith and trust in Christ. In His words, "I am in My Father, and you in Me, and I in you."

This is an awesome thought. The One who put the stars in space and created all things with the power of His spoken word is alive in me. He is in the Father, and I am in Him—but not only that, I also have the Holy Spirit in me to lead and guide me through anything and everything life will bring my way. Eureka!

11   SPRING UP, O WELL

*W*hile it is one thing to grasp the fact that the Holy Spirit is *in you*, the real secret to victorious living is understanding that He also desires to live *through you*. When you allow Him to live through you, you become a blessing to others by showing the world a picture of the Christ who has taken up residency in your heart. On a hot midday in Samaria, Jesus promised a woman He met at a well that if she trusted in Him, she would never thirst for the things of the world again and that she would have within her "a well of water springing up into everlasting life" (John 4:14 KJV). Later, back in Jerusalem on the feast day, He promised to all in His hearing that if any single one of them would believe in Him, then "out of his heart will flow rivers of living water" (John 7:38). God's plain desire is that this "well of water" within us would flow like "rivers of living water" through us.

As previously mentioned, every summer during my boyhood days, our family traveled from Texas to the Smoky

Mountains of Tennessee. For several days we would visit various relatives in that beautiful part of the country. My favorite relatives were my great-uncle Lester and his wife, Idelle. They owned and operated a little one-room country store in a mountain hamlet nine miles outside of Pikeville. Hence, the community was named Nine Mile. Even as I write these words, I can still smell the cedar being whittled on the store's front porch bench by a couple of old-timers who passed the time of day there. My uncle's home was adjacent to the little store, and one of the novelties of the day for this little city boy was the fact that, way up in those Tennessee hills, their home had no running water.

Outside the back door of the house was an old surface-pump well. To draw water, you had to take a little water from the mason jar that always sat nearby and pour it in to the pump in order to prime it. Then you would take the long handle and pump . . . pump . . . pump . . . pump until the water started flowing up through the spout from the well below. As long as you kept pumping, the water flowed in a steady stream. But the moment you stopped rigorously pumping the handle, the flow of water would cease. It was a lot of work.

There is another kind of well, though. It is called an *artesian well*. This well is dug much deeper into the ground until it hits an underground river or stream. You never have to pump an artesian well. You simply tap into it, attach a faucet, turn on the spigot, and the water just flows and flows.

> Some people want to be served, but those living in the fullness of the Holy Spirit want to serve by allowing the Spirit to flow through them.

There are a lot of believers who are like my great-uncle's old surface-pump well. They are a bit shallow, and to get them to serve the Lord, you always have to prime the pump. Then you have to pump . . . pump . . . pump. As long as you keep pumping, encouraging, motivating, and patting them on the back, they remain in service. But the moment you quit, they cease to serve. On the other hand, there are believers who have tapped deep into what Jesus called "rivers of living water" and are continuously filled with the Spirit. Their lives overflow with His fullness. Some people want to be served, but those living in the fullness of the Holy Spirit want to serve by allowing the Spirit to flow through them.

Many people who have traveled to Israel have seen the most beautiful word picture of this truth in the two bodies of water within the Holy Land. In the north, the Sea of Galilee is crystal clear, a beautiful blue, and teeming with life. The Jordan River's headwaters flow south from myriad streams near Mount Hermon and empty into the Sea of Galilee. From the southern end of the sea, the river finds its outlet and continues its journey south some seventy miles until it empties into the Dead Sea. The Dead Sea has earned its name for a reason. It is dead. With no aquatic life found in its waters, the sulfuric smell arising from it can be nauseating.

What is the difference between these two bodies of water? The Dead Sea has no outlet. It takes in fresh water, but it gives nothing out. On the other hand, the Sea of Galilee has both an inlet and an outlet. It allows the fresh water it receives to flow through it and out the other end. So it is with the vibrant, victorious believer in Christ who not only receives God's fullness but also gives it away. Just like the Sea of Galilee, that believer is continually refilled with the Holy Spirit.

The Lord wants to make you a channel of His blessing today so that the Holy Spirit who is in you will flow through you to those who are thirsting for more in life. The Holy Spirit wants to be in you "a well of water springing up into everlasting life" (John 4:14 KJV). You were never designed to become a shallow service well that has to be pumped up all the time to get you to flow. You were meant to be an artesian well, dug deep into the soil of God's good grace. Turn on the faucet and let it flow.

12 FILL MY CUP, LORD

One of my favorite and most frequently sung choruses of my young Christian life was "Fill My Cup, Lord," written by Richard Blanchard, a Methodist minister, and made widely popular by such groups as the Gaithers. The song painted a word picture of our being like a cup that, when cleaned out, the Holy Spirit would come and fill to the brim. The more I sang that chorus and the more I got to know the Holy Spirit, the more I understood that He is a person, not a substance, and the real secret to being filled with the Holy Spirit is not in getting more of Him but in giving Him more of me. I started thinking of my relationship with Him more in terms of a garden hose that was continuing to fill me and flowing through me and out of me to bless others rather than as some cup that needed to be filled for my own benefit. It is one thing to have the Holy Spirit in us and another to allow Him to flow through us.

We read over and over in Scripture of men and women who were filled with the Holy Spirit in such a manner.

Stephen was the first Christian martyr, stoned outside the Lions' Gate of the old city of Jerusalem. When he was appointed one of the first deacons in the early church, the Bible records he was "a man full of faith and the Holy Spirit" (Acts 6:5). In fact, he was so on fire that he caught the attention of the religious authorities and was brought to trial before the high priest and the council. As he spoke in response to their accusations, we're told that the people there "saw his face as the face of an angel" (Acts 6:15). In the next chapter, as he was being stoned to death, Scripture records that Stephen, "being full of the Holy Spirit, gazed into heaven and saw the glory of God, and Jesus standing at the right hand of God" (Acts 7:55).

This filling of the Holy Spirit was not limited to a few good people. Acts 11:24 tells us that Barnabas was "a good man, full of the Holy Spirit and of faith," and later we read that "the disciples were filled with joy and with the Holy Spirit" (Acts 13:52). It is one thing to have the Holy Spirit *in us* and quite another for Him to have us so that He might fill us and flow *through us*.

But what exactly is commanded of us in Scripture with reference to the Holy Spirit? Is it to be sealed with the Holy Spirit? No. The Bible says, "In Him you also trusted, after you heard the word of truth, the gospel of your salvation;

> If you have trusted in Christ, you have been sealed with the Holy Spirit, now and forever.

in whom also, having believed, you were sealed with the Holy Spirit of promise" (Ephesians 1:13). This is not a command. Being sealed with the Holy Spirit is a gift from God to you at salvation to keep you in the faith. If you have trusted in Christ, you have been sealed with the Holy Spirit, now and forever.

Is the command then to be indwelt by the Holy Spirit? This again is not a command. If you have trusted in Christ to save you, He has already sent the Holy Spirit to live in you and indwell you now and forever. The apostle Paul instructed that "your body is the temple of the Holy Spirit who is in you" (1 Corinthians 6:19). In fact, in the greatest theological treatise ever written, Paul warns that "if anyone does not have the Spirit of Christ, he is not His" (Romans 8:9).

We are not commanded to be sealed with the Holy Spirit. We have been sealed already. We are not commanded to be indwelt with the Holy Spirit. He is alive and living within every believer from the moment of belief.

The only directive, the only *command* regarding the Holy Spirit, is found in Ephesians 5:18, where Scripture mandates that we "be filled with the Spirit." This is not an option for the believer, yet it is something that few seem to give much thought to. God commands us to be filled with His Spirit. When we awaken to the reality that the Holy Spirit is alive today in us, then it should make sense that we allow Him to fill us with His fullness so that the overflow of His life in us might flow through us to all around.

There are three steps to being filled with the Holy Spirit. We are to confess our sins to Him, crown Him as Lord, and claim Him and His truth as our own.

First, *confess* your sins to Him. Come clean before Him. The Spirit cannot fill a dirty vessel. We have a precious promise: "If we confess our sins, He is faithful and just to forgive us our sins and to cleanse us from all unrighteousness" (1 John 1:9). To confess means to say the same as God says about your sin. It is not just some little vice to laugh off. It cannot be excused by saying everyone else is doing it. It cannot be minimized by claiming it is not as bad as the sin of other people you know. Our sin—yours and mine—is so serious it put Christ on the cross. So, step one: Confess your sin.

Next, *crown* Jesus Christ as Lord of your life. Take yourself off the throne of your heart and put Him there by an act of your faith. "For to this end Christ died and rose and lived again, that He might be Lord of both the

> Crown Jesus Christ as Lord of your life. Take yourself off the throne of your heart and put Him there by an act of your faith.

dead and the living" (Romans 14:9). You can't *make* Jesus Lord of your life—He is already Lord, whether you recognize it or not. But you can acknowledge Him as Lord. Move off your lofty throne and allow Him to reign and rule from your heart.

Finally, through faith, *claim* Him as your own. The fact that He indwells and fills you means that you can claim the amazing promise Jesus made in Mark 11:24 when He said, "Whatever things you ask when you pray, believe that you receive them, and you will have them."

What is more important to you—what God says or how you feel? Give that serious thought. You are filled by faith in Him. Faith does not *bring* the victory in Christian living. Faith *is* the victory! So go ahead. Confess, crown, and claim the Holy Spirit's filling by faith. Then it might be said of you what was said of Jesus' followers: "The disciples were filled with joy and with the Holy Spirit" (Acts 13:52).

13 BE FILLED

*A*s we discussed earlier, there is only one commandment in all the Bible related to our relationship with the Holy Spirit. It is found in Paul's letter to the Ephesians: "Do not be drunk with wine, in which is dissipation; but be filled with the Spirit" (Ephesians 5:18). Being filled with the Holy Spirit is not an option for the believer. It is imperative for Christian living. Every verb has a number, a tense, a voice, and a mood. When dissecting this phrase—"be filled"—in its original language, we find that the number is plural, meaning everyone, all of us. The tense is present, meaning it is to be a continual, ongoing action, not a one-time event. The voice is passive, which indicates that the subject does not act in and of itself; it is acted upon by another. Finally, the phrase is presented in the imperative mood, signifying that it is not a suggestion

> Ephesians 5:18 can more directly be translated as "all of us must always be actively being filled with the Spirit."

or something to think about; it is a mandate, a command to incorporate. Putting this all together then, we find that Ephesians 5:18 can more directly be translated as "all of us must always be actively being filled with the Spirit."

The Bible draws a stark contrast between the negative admonition to "not be drunk with wine" and the positive command to "be filled with the Spirit." I have found, however, that there is not much balance in the emphasis between these two commands in many of our evangelical circles. We have made much of not drinking alcohol and perhaps too little of living the Spirit-filled life. When I went to my first pastorate in Hobart, Oklahoma, I was met with a controversy over the actions of a deacon. Someone had seen him at a restaurant up in Oklahoma City with a glass of wine in front of him. In a deacons' meeting before I arrived on the scene, they had made much of this, booting him off the deacon board and publicly bringing the matter before the church. I had not been there long, however, before I discovered that some of those same deacons were a lot more concerned with the first part of Ephesians 5:18, being "drunk with wine," than they were with the rest of the sentence, "be filled with the Spirit." I wondered what would have happened if we were as vigilant about those deacons who were obviously not filled with the

Spirit as we were with the one who drank a glass of wine with his meal.

The positive command to be filled with the Spirit of God should be just as important to us as the negative one not to be drunk with alcoholic beverages. Think about it. Next Sunday, what would happen if the preacher stumbled up to the pulpit, stammered through the reading of the Scripture with a slurred voice while staggering to and fro from one side of the pulpit to the other? A drunk preacher is in no condition to preach—we can all agree on that. But that is only half the story. A preacher who is not filled with the Spirit of God is equally in no condition to stand behind the sacred desk or preach.

> The positive command to be filled with the Spirit of God should be just as important to us as the negative one not to be drunk with alcoholic beverages.

What if a singer stood to sing a solo before the message and wobbled back and forth missing some of the words while in a drunken stupor? He or she would be in no condition to lead worship. Neither would someone be in a condition to lead worship if he or she were not being filled with the Spirit of God. It is just as wrong for a person not to be filled with the Spirit as it is to be drunk with wine.

In fact, far more havoc has been created in churches by leaders who were not being filled with God's Spirit as they led than by those who drank wine. At least you can smell a drunk when he or she is sitting by you. It is not always as obvious that someone is not being filled with the Spirit.

Much of the issue with many today is found in two words—influence and power. Look at the early believers in Jerusalem. They had little influence with the rulers of the day. They didn't focus on the social ills around them, nor did they seek to influence the Roman government through petitions and pickets. They did not have pictures on their walls of themselves with the Caesar or the governor or the puppet Jewish ruler. They had little political capital and zero influence with virtually anyone. They did not even have enough influence to keep Peter out of prison. But they had enough power to pray him out (Acts 12)!

What a difference the church could make in our world if we rediscovered the difference between having influence and having spiritual power by being filled with the Spirit. The result of the Spirit's fullness in our lives is always a new source of power. Jesus said, "You shall receive power." When? "When the Holy Spirit has come upon you" (Acts 1:8).

When we are not being filled with God's Spirit, we

grieve Him. The Bible admonishes us, "Do not grieve the Holy Spirit of God, by whom you were sealed for the day of redemption" (Ephesians 4:30). Most of us have at some point in life experienced real grief and can remember the emotion it brings. But did you know that when we are not allowing the Spirit to control every aspect of our lives, we are grieving Him? We can also quench His work when we do not allow Him to fill us with His presence and power. We are admonished not to "quench" the Holy Spirit (1 Thessalonians 5:19). That means a person who is not filled with God's fullness can actually quench or stymie the work of God in themself or in others.

God's desire is that in place of always trying to get more of Him (remember He is a person, not a substance), we instead give Him more of us, daily surrendering every area of our lives to His Lordship, coming clean in daily confession, crowning Him as Lord of all, and claiming His promise that we can be filled by faith. Our greatest need is power to overcome and live in victory, and the same Spirit who raised Christ from the dead lives in me and in you. As a believer you have no more option in being filled than you do in whether you will make your house payment or pay your taxes. It is God's command: "Be filled with the Spirit!" (Ephesians 5:18).

14 PROVE IT!

*W*e live in a "prove it" culture. "Show me." "Let me see it." "I need proof!" These are common responses to claims made by Christ followers. What evidence, then, what proof do we have that we are being filled with the Holy Spirit?

Some would say the proof is found in our being able to perform certain supernatural, spiritual gifts. Yet we can read the lengthiest passage in all the Bible on spiritual gifts (1 Corinthians 12–14) and not find a single syllable about any of the gifts serving as indicators of the Spirit's fullness in our lives. In fact, the spiritual gifts are not a sign of spiritual maturity at all. Paul admonished the believers in Corinth (and us) because he "could not speak to [them] as to spiritual people but as to carnal, as to babes in Christ" (1 Corinthians 3:1).

The more we study the Bible, the more we understand the importance of context. It is often said that a text without a context is simply a pretext. Look at the context in which the Bible commands us to "be filled with the Spirit" (Ephesians 5:18). Read on in your Bible. There is no period at the end of verse 18. There is a comma, which tells us to read on within the context of what the Holy Spirit is saying through the Bible writer. When we continue reading, we do not find a period indicating the conclusion of the thought until we come to the end of verse 21.

The three verses following Ephesians 5:18 show us the evidence, the proof that we are being filled with the Spirit of God. There is an *inward* evidence in verse 19: "singing and making melody in your heart." There is an *upward* evidence in verse 20: "giving thanks always for all things to God the Father in the name of our Lord Jesus Christ." And finally, there is an *outward* evidence in verse 21: "submitting to one another in the fear of God." After all that, then comes the period!

When we boil it all down, life is about relationships. There are three types of relationships in life. There is the outward expression of relationship. That is, we have a relationship with others at home, at the office, in the social arena, or wherever. We were created to connect with one another in these outward interpersonal relationships. Back in the very beginning of the entire created order, God paused and spoke after each creative act. Do you remember what He said? "*That's good*" (my paraphrase). He said this when He made the sun, the moon, and the stars and put them in their places, and they run in clocklike precision to this very day. He divided the sea and land, spoke vegetation and animal life into existence, and at the end of each act declared, "That's good." Then He made man. And when He did, God said something else—*not* good! "It is not good that man should be alone" (Genesis 2:18). We were made to connect with one another in the power of positive and productive interpersonal relationships. This is the outward connection.

> We were made to connect with one another in the power of positive and productive interpersonal relationships.

Second, we have a relationship with ourselves. This is the inward connection. We may call it self-esteem, self-respect, or self-worth. We get up each morning, look at ourselves in the mirror, and go on to live each day with ourselves. The problems that arise in our outward relationships are often a direct result of what is going on within us. When we are angry within, we are likely to project that anger onto those we love the most. We not only have to relate to others, but we must be properly related to ourselves.

The third relationship we can have is the upward relationship. This is what separates us from all other created order, and it is an awesome reality. We have the capacity to enter into a relationship with Jesus Christ and, through the Holy Spirit who comes to take up residency in us, to know God in the relationship of Father and child.

What is the bottom line then? We will never be properly related to others until we are properly related to ourselves. And this cannot fully happen until we come into relationship with Jesus Christ and find our self-worth in Him, mirroring in our own lives the riches that Paul described, the "glory of this mystery . . . which is Christ in you, the hope of glory" (Colossians 1:27).

Two thousand years ago, the apostle Paul laid hold of this threefold principle of relationship and, under the direction of the Holy Spirit, masterfully framed it as the proof that the Holy Spirit was not simply *living* in us but *filling* us with His person and presence. Ephesians 5:19 provides the inward evidence of His filling. How can you know that you are being filled with the Spirit? You will have a song in your heart that fills you with inner joy. Ephesians 5:20 provides the upward evidence. How does God know that you are being filled? Of course, He knows everything and never needs proof, but the evidence you can see will be that you are living your life with gratitude, giving thanks to Him at all times for all things.

Finally, Ephesians 5:21 provides the outward evidence. How do others with whom you come in contact know you are a Spirit-filled believer? Through your submission of yourself to others as you "esteem others better than [your]self" (Philippians 2:3). The evidence is that you do not always have to get your way or be the center of attention. Instead, you live with a humble spirit toward those around you.

When you evidence these things in your life, you are the proof that Jesus is not just real but alive today! And when you live this way, others will take note, and God will receive glory. As the old adage says, "The proof is in the pudding."

15 AN INWARD EVIDENCE

*H*ow will you know within yourself that you are being filled with God's Spirit? As we have seen, His command is that we "be filled with the Holy Spirit" (Ephesians 5:18). The next verse provides the evidence you need: "speaking to one another in psalms and hymns and spiritual songs, singing and making melody in your heart to the Lord" (Ephesians 5:19). You will "rejoice with joy unspeakable and full of glory" (1 Peter 1:8 KJV).

Keeping a song in your heart is the inward evidence. You cannot stay filled with the Spirit without manifesting this joy from within. That inward spirit is what distinguishes the Christian faith from all other religions. We are not a religion; we are about a living and vibrant relationship that puts joy in our hearts despite the circumstances that come our way. People of other faiths may have impressive temples and mosques, mantras and chants, but they have no song in their hearts. When we are being filled with God's Spirit, the first evidence is an inward joy that puts a song of praise within.

When the Spirit is filling your life, you are happy on the inside, even when things aren't going the way you wish they would on the outside. Look at Paul and Silas in Acts 16:22–40. They were beaten until their backs were bloody pulps and then thrown into the inner sanctum of a wretched Philippian jail. We might expect them to feel sorry for themselves, to complain about their unfair and unjust situation, to wonder where God was in light of it all. But what did they do when the midnight hour came? "At midnight Paul and Silas were praying and singing hymns to God, and the prisoners were listening to them" (Acts 16:25). They were filled with the Spirit of God, and in their darkest hour, they still had a song of praise to Him in their hearts.

> When the Spirit is filling your life, you are happy on the inside, even when things aren't going the way you wish they would on the outside.

Note that this song is found "in your heart." I am so glad the instrument of our praise, the proof of our filling, is not evidenced in our vocal cords but in our hearts. I cannot carry a tune and I cannot sing in harmony, but I sure can keep a song where it matters most, in my heart. When our hearts are not right—when we are on the thrones of our lives—our songs will not be pleasing to the Lord. This is the inward evidence. You will know. You will have a song, not necessarily coming forth from your mouth, but deep within your heart where it really matters.

It is also important to know to whom your song should be directed. Sing "in your heart to the Lord" (Ephesians 5:19). The Holy Spirit is in the world to glorify the Lord Jesus Christ. He is not here to glorify us before other people. Our songs are to be sung to an audience of One, the Lord Jesus Christ. Christian music was never intended to be used for performance. In fact, it was not designed by God to be a tool of evangelism. It is not intended for the world. It is to be directed in praise *to the Lord.*

How will you know that God's Spirit is filling you? You will have a joyous song, not necessarily coming from your lips but bubbling deep within. You can't help but be "singing and making melody in your heart to the Lord." In the traffic patterns of your life, when you hear a song (on the radio or perhaps when you're on hold on the telephone or in an elevator), let it remind you of the inward evidence of God's Spirit working in your heart.

16 AN UPWARD EVIDENCE

*I*n addition to the inward evidence of the Spirit filling our lives, there is upward evidence as well. Ephesians 5:20 says the Spirit-filled believer will be "giving thanks always for all things to God the Father in the name of our Lord Jesus Christ." Note that our thanks are to be directed primarily to God the Father. When we realize that He is the source of everything and we allow His Spirit to fill us, our hearts cannot help but be filled with thanksgiving to Him "always for all things." The Bible says, "Every good gift and every perfect gift is from above, and comes down from the Father of lights, with whom is no shadow of turning" (James 1:17).

Paul states that the proof of the filling is a spirit of thanksgiving to God. When? Always! I can almost sense what some are thinking now. *Always? But you don't know my problem.* Or *You don't know my spouse.* Someone may be saying to themselves, *You don't know the situation I am faced with at the moment.* You are right. I don't know. But

God does. God knows all about you. And this verse still says to give thanks always for all things. We can be thankful because, if we are being filled with His fullness, we have the confidence that He has not abdicated His throne; therefore, we rest in the fact that He is in control always of all things.

You may be searching for God's will in a difficult situation. Everything written in Ephesians 5:18–20 is preceded and predicated by verse 17: "Therefore do not be unwise, but understand what *the will of the Lord* is" (emphasis added). Understanding the will of the Lord flows right into being filled with the Spirit in verse 18 and on into giving thanks always for all things in verse 20. A thankful heart is the place to begin finding the will of God. The Bible says, "In everything give thanks; *for this is the will of God* in Christ Jesus for you" (1 Thessalonians 5:18, emphasis added).

> A thankful heart is the place to begin finding the will of God.

It is one thing to give thanks "always" but another to give thanks for "all things." Most of our prayers of thanksgiving come after we receive some unexpected blessing or when some immediate need is met supernaturally or we are healed from a sickness. But the proof of the Spirit's

83

fullness in our lives is that we give thanks for "all things," not just the blessings that come our way. Being thankful means we do not only acknowledge gratitude before or after a circumstance of life but even in the middle of unpleasant things. The evidence is found in a prayer that says, "Lord, I don't understand it, but I thank You for Your promise that all things are working together for good to those of us who love You and are called to your purpose" (Romans 8:28).

God allows various things to happen in life that He uses to perfect our faith. The disciples could attest to this. One evening they were where God told them to be (in the boat) and doing what God told them to do (go to the other side of the lake) (Matthew 14:22–24). They were in the middle of God's will and still got caught in a storm. When they panicked, He came walking to them on the water, calmed the storm, and got into the boat with them. Then He said, "O you of little faith, why did you doubt?" (v. 31). He then used the storm to teach them a valuable life lesson and, in doing so, He perfected their faith.

There are two kinds of storms that come our way in life. There are *storms of perfection* and *storms of correction*. The disciples' storm was one of perfection. The prophet Jonah, however, found himself in a different situation.

God had instructed him to go in one direction but, unlike the disciples on the Sea of Galilee, Jonah headed in the opposite direction. Because of his direct disobedience, he wound up on a ship in a storm at sea, during which he was thrown overboard and swallowed by a great fish. Jonah's was not a storm of perfection but a storm of correction. Storms of correction come when we are out of the will of God.

Jonah spent the next three days and three nights in the belly of that fish with lots of time to reflect on the choices he had made. Would he ever be delivered? Finally, Jonah 2:9 says that "with the voice of thanksgiving" he offered a prayer to God from inside the fish. He began to thank God for all things, and the very next verse states "So the LORD spoke to the fish, and it vomited Jonah onto dry land" (Jonah 2:10). The act of giving thanks "always and in all things" can have a liberating effect on all of us.

> The act of giving thanks "always and in all things" can have a liberating effect on all of us.

The fullness of God in our lives is proven by our ability to thank God in all things. There is a difference between those believers who walk by sight and those who walk by faith. Those who walk by sight can sing songs of praise and offer thanksgiving only after their deliverance comes. Those who walk by faith and are filled with the Spirit choose to live in a spirit of thanksgiving even in the face of adversity. The Bible says, "Those who sacrifice thank offerings honor me, and to the blameless I will show my salvation" (Psalm 50:23 NIV).

Giving thanks is the upward evidence you present to God that reveals His fullness in your life. Yes, "in everything give thanks; for this is the will of God in Christ Jesus for you" (1 Thessalonians 5:18). If you are searching for the will of God in a matter, giving thanks is a good place to start.

17 AN OUTWARD EVIDENCE

*T*he person being filled with the Holy Spirit will never have to advertise it. There is not just an inward evidence and an upward evidence but an outward one as well. It will be obvious to those with whom you come in contact. How will others know? Paul continued by saying we will submit "to one another in the fear of God" (Ephesians 5:21). That is to say, it will be apparent as we esteem other people better than ourselves and with humility put them before us. It is not only the things we say or the way we say them that lets others know we are filled with God's Holy Spirit; rather, it is in how we behave in our relationships with others that reveals the Spirit's work within us.

The words *submit* and *submission* have become anathema to many in our modern culture, due in large part to the way the concept is often presented and the connotation it has earned in some circles. But *submission* is a beautiful word when understood in its biblical context.

It has nothing to do with inferiority. We see it in the military. Soldiers live in submission to their commanding officers. When people join the army, they relinquish some control over their lives. They do not get out of bed in the morning whenever they feel like it. They can't just take a few days off when they want to. They become people under authority. In the eyes of God, we are all equal. Submission means one places himself or herself in submission to another. Those who are being filled with God's Spirit do voluntarily what the soldier does by command.

Paul described it best for the believer by saying:

Let each of you look out not only for his own interests, but also for the interests of others. Let this mind be in you which was also in Christ Jesus, who, being in the form of God, did not consider it robbery to be equal with God, but made Himself of no reputation, taking the form of a bondservant, and coming in the likeness of men. And being found in appearance as a man, He humbled Himself and became obedient to the point of death, even the death of the cross." (Philippians 2:4–8)

As in everything, Christ is our example. We see it best on the evening of the crucifixion. When He had gathered the disciples in the upper room on Mount Zion, He rose from the Passover table, girded Himself with a towel, and kneeling before each of the twelve, He began to wash their feet. And then, with His gaze penetrating their hearts, He said, "If I then, your Lord and Teacher, have washed your feet, you also ought to wash one another's feet. For I have given you an example, that you should do as I have done to you" (John 13:14–15).

Through this act and these words, Jesus conveyed that the greatest of people are the ones who use their authority to build up those around them instead of promoting themselves. There is only one way we can submit to one another like this, and that is by being filled with the Spirit. It is not in us to do this on our own because when we live in the flesh, we become consumed with self-seeking and self-centeredness.

This outward evidence is a mutual submission to "one another." For example, my wife is not just submitted to me; I am submitted to her as well. I don't just go out at night on my own. I don't take off on a trip without her knowledge. We live in mutual submission to each other. It is in this relationship of mutual submission that King Solomon admonished us, saying, "The discretion of a man makes him slow to anger, and his glory is to overlook a transgression" (Proverbs 19:11). If more of us took this wisdom to heart, mutual submission would become as natural as water running downhill, especially when we manifest the power of the Holy Spirit filling us with His fullness. When we realize that we are nothing without Christ and when we are filled with the Spirit and take up our own cross and follow Him, we become dead to self and to sin. Mutual submission to one another then becomes a lifestyle. Jesus said, "If anyone desires to come after Me, let him . . . take up his cross daily, and follow Me" (Luke 9:23). In the first-century world, if a person was seen carrying a cross, everyone knew that person was going to die. Jesus said we should live like a dead person—if we are dead to our sin and self, then mutual submission will not be problematic. It is the outward evidence of the filling of the Spirit in our lives.

After all, we are all members of one body, the body of Christ. Members of my own body function by being in submission to one another. When my brain sends a message to my hand to pick up something, it submits. In like manner, that is God's divine intention for His own body, the church—you and me. We have a command: be filled with the Spirit. There is an inward evidence—we will have a song in our hearts. There is an upward evidence—we will give thanks always for all things. And there is an outward evidence that allows others to know without our telling them or advertising it. We will submit to one another in the fear of the Lord.

18 AN IMPORTANT ENVIRONMENT

*B*efore we leave these principles and proofs of the fullness of the Holy Spirit in our lives, there is one more important word. Note the way the entire discourse in Ephesians 5:17–21 ends—"submitting to one another *in the fear of God*" (emphasis added). The phrase "in the fear of God" is not some little tagline stuck on the end of these words concerning the fullness of the Holy Spirit. It is the key to understanding it all. All of the above—the Spirit's fullness in our lives, a song in our heart, a spirit of thanksgiving, and a mutual submission to one another—is to be carried out in the environment of each of us living in "the fear of God."

We are to live with a song in our hearts not simply to have a happy disposition but because of the fear of God. We are to always offer thanksgiving to Him not because it can mean deliverance for us as it did for Jonah, but because of the fear of God. We are to live in mutual submission with our spouses and friends not because it brings peace but because of the fear of God. Our entire being is to be lived in the environment of the fear of God. Verses 18 through 21 have flowed naturally with all commas until this point. Verse 21 brings Paul's teaching to a full stop, finally placing a period after the phrase "in the fear of God." But who of us is doing this today? Who of us can even define what it means to live in the fear of God?

Perhaps no Christian discipline is as forgotten as the idea of living in the fear of the Lord. Yet this theme is woven like a thread through the pages of Scripture as it showcases men and women who lived with the power of the Holy Spirit in them. To name just a few, we can start with Noah, who "moved with godly fear" as he built the ark (Hebrews 11:7).

> Perhaps no Christian discipline is as forgotten as the idea of living in the fear of the Lord.

When Moses ascended Mount Nebo, where he went to die, he left the Israelites (who, after forty years of wandering, were finally about to enter the Promised Land) with this question: "What does the LORD your God require of you, but to fear the LORD your God" (Deuteronomy 10:12). And what about the Proverbs 31 woman? If you are interested in knowing her secret, read on into chapter 31 until you come to verse 30: "A woman who fears the LORD, she shall be praised."

The same holds true throughout the Gospels. The young Virgin Mary praised God, saying, "His mercy is on those who fear Him" (Luke 1:50). In Acts we find reference by the early believers to the fear of the Lord on almost every page. We read that when the Holy Spirit came on the day of Pentecost, they "continued steadfastly . . . [and] fear came upon every soul" (Acts 2:42–43). The epistles are replete with the same theme. In Romans 3:18, Paul lamented a people who had "no fear of God before their eyes." And in the Ephesian discourse before us, he reminded us to submit to one another "in the fear of God" (Ephesians 5:21). Finally, in the book of Revelation, John reported that in the middle of a great praise service in heaven, he heard a loud voice coming from God's throne, saying, "Praise our God, all you His servants and those who fear Him" (Revelation 19:5).

How can it be that this common theme throughout the Bible is a forgotten concept for so many believers today? What does it really mean to live in an environment of the fear of the Lord? Does it mean we are to live our lives in constant fright or flight, concerned that if we do or say something wrong, God will zap us with His hand of retribution? No. Nothing could be further from biblical truth.

Living in the fear of God is not living with the fear that God might put His hand of retribution upon us in discipline. It is the fear that God might take His hand *off* us—His hand of protection, His hand of blessing, His hand of anointing. Living the Spirit-filled life means we have a conscious awareness of His continual presence, and we do not want to do anything that would cause God to take His hand of anointing off us. When we begin to live in this environment, it makes a difference in where we go, what we watch, what we say, and how we live.

How do we begin to live in this new dimension? We start at the same place we begin everything in the Christian life—with the Word of God. King Solomon advised, "If you receive my words, and treasure my commands within you, so that you incline your ear to wisdom, and apply your heart to understanding . . . then you will understand the fear of the LORD" (Proverbs 2:1–2, 5). Living in the fear of God is a learned behavior as we remain immersed in His Word and consciously aware of His presence.

The prophet Isaiah asked a question over 2,500 years ago that still convicts and provokes thought today: "Who among you fears the LORD?" (Isaiah 50:10). When you begin to live in this environment, you will discover that "the secret of the LORD is with those who fear Him" (Psalm 25:14).

We have a command from God: "Be filled with the Holy Spirit" (Ephesians 5:18). When we are, we will find ourselves with a song in our hearts, an attitude of thanksgiving to God, and a mutual spirit of submission with others. But remember, it is all to be done within the atmosphere and environment of the fear of God. And now it is time to put a period at the end of this long sentence.

19 YOU ARE GIFTED

*Y*ou are gifted. Maybe no one has ever said that to you before, but it is true. Every believer has at least one spiritual gift bestowed upon them from God "for the profit of all" (1 Corinthians 12:7). The apostle Paul addressed the topic of spiritual gifts in 1 Corinthians chapters 12 through 14, beginning with this statement: "Now concerning spiritual gifts, . . . I do not want you to be ignorant" (1 Corinthians 12:1). And yet, if you want to enter into an uninformed conversation, just ask many believers about the what, how, and why of their own spiritual gift.

At the outset we should understand that there is a difference between the "gift of the Holy Spirit" and the "gifts of the Holy Spirit." The *gift* is the Holy Spirit Himself, given to us when we begin our journey of the Christian life through repentance and faith in Christ. We receive this gift of the Holy Spirit at the moment of our conversion. The Holy Spirit is God's birthday gift to us as He comes to live in us, never to leave us, and to empower us for service.

As Peter called people to repent and trust in Christ, he said they would "receive the gift of the Holy Spirit" (Acts 2:38).

The *gifts of the Spirit*, on the other hand, are special endowments for service in the body of Christ that God gives to us. Everyone has at least one gift. No one has all the gifts.

> The *gifts of the Spirit* . . . are special endowments for service in the body of Christ that God gives to us. Everyone has at least one gift.

There is some concern in modern Christianity over the word *charisma*. Generally speaking, someone might be said to have charisma or a charismatic presence. This simply means they have a winsome charm about them that is attractive to other people. In the New Testament this word is most often used to describe the supernatural gifts that God bestows upon His children. The word *charisma* (plural *charismata*) is derived from the Greek word for grace, *charis*. Charismata, in the language of the Bible, literally means "a gift of grace."

In our church world today, however, there are some who have exchanged the word *charisma* for what I will call *charisphobia*. That is, they seem to fear these gifts of grace and avoid the mention of them altogether. In contrast, others suffer from what might be called *charismania*.

They've become so consumed with the supernatural and certain gifts that manifest themselves in miracles that in some cases the *gift Himself* is overtaken. But I will say that every believer in Christ is a charismatic, meaning they have a spiritual gift, sovereignly bestowed upon them from God for the edification and the building up of the body of Christ.

> Every believer in Christ is a charismatic, meaning they have a spiritual gift, sovereignly bestowed upon them from God for the edification and the building up of the body of Christ.

In the body of Christ, we are not just dependent upon Him but also upon each other. We are members of one body. For thirty-three years, the world looked upon the physical body of Christ. He walked among us, spoke the greatest words ever spoken, touched people with His hands of mercy, and then offered Himself as the final and complete sacrifice for our sins. Then He was buried, arose, and ascended back to the Father. Today, we—you and I—are the visible body of Christ, the picture of Him to a lost and dying world. We are "all the members of that one body" (1 Corinthians 12:12).

The parts of our physical bodies work in tandem to carry out our desires. When the brain sends a signal to your hand to pick up a book, your hand works together with other parts of your body to accomplish the task. It is the same with the body of Christ. Paul made it clear:

> For as the body is one and has many members, but all the members of that one body, being many, are one body, so also is Christ. For by one Spirit we were all baptized into one body—whether Jews or Greeks, whether slaves or free—and have all been made to drink into one Spirit. For in fact the body is not one member but many. . . . Now you are the body of Christ, and members individually. (1 Corinthians 12:12–14, 27)

Everyone is important in the body of Christ. In biological, physical terms, your health and well-being hinges on the health and well-being of every single part of your body. When one body part is injured or infected, it limits the effectiveness of your entire body. In some cases, one part of your body can shut down your entire system. Paul framed it like this in verse 21: "The eye cannot say to the hand, 'I have no need of you'; nor again the head to the feet, 'I have no need of you.'" The same is true of Christ's body—you, me, and all believers. One believer cannot say to another, "I have no need of you. I will be fine without you." We need each other, all of us in the body of Christ. Paul went on to say, "There should be no schism in the body, but that the members should have the same care for one another. And if one member suffers, all the members suffer with it" (1 Corinthians 12:25–26).

God has gifted each member of the body of Christ with particular gifts, not for self-glorification but for the good health of His entire body. Some have service gifts like gifts of mercy, teaching, faith, giving, and the like. Some have been given particular sign gifts, the gifts of healing or miracles, for example. There are also gifts designed specifically to equip the church, like evangelism or the gift of the pastor-teacher. There are a multitude of gifts given to us by God.

These gifts of grace are not rewards. Neither are they natural abilities that we may or may not already possess. They are supernatural gifts distributed to us in God's perfect wisdom. The church is supernatural, not just in its origin but in its operation. I once heard Vance Havner, a revivalist of a past generation, say, "The church has to be supernatural because anything else could not exist this long the way we are running it." One must wonder whether, if the Holy Spirit were to withdraw from some churches today, they would simply go on functioning as always with their own plans and programs. If what is happening in your church is not supernatural, it just might be superficial.

You are gifted. You have a specific gift of grace given to you from God. When you operate within that gift, you serve to build up Christ's own body on earth. What is your spiritual gift? If you do not know, you are about to find out. Let's turn the page and discover your special God-given gift. You will recognize it because it is the thing you love to do; it is what energizes you; in fact, it is the very thing in which you find your greatest joy. When you discover it, the body of Christ will use it, and God will be glorified by your use of it.

20 IT'S TIME TO DISCOVER YOUR GIFT

*M*ost of us have had to say goodbye to someone we love. Perhaps it happened at an airport when that person was moving to another part of the country or across the world and you watched and waved until the plane was out of sight. Maybe it was the goodbye you gave your child as you dropped them off at college for the first time and drove away, your eyes watching the rearview mirror for a final glance. Many of us have said goodbye at the deathbed of our mom or dad or other loved ones. Saying goodbye to someone close to us is one of the more difficult experiences of life.

The disciples had such an experience. They had been with Jesus for over three years in the Galilean mountains and walking the dusty trails of Judea. They had slept with Him every night and eaten a thousand meals together. Then came the time to say goodbye. He led them up the Mount of Olives as far as the little village of Bethany, then

Scripture records, "It came to pass, while He blessed them, that He was parted from them and carried up into heaven" (Luke 24:51). You would think they must have been devastated and in despair. But no. The very next verse says, "And they worshiped Him, and returned to Jerusalem with great joy" (Luke 24:52).

What? He was gone! And yet, they went back to the very city where He had been so cruelly crucified and did so "with great joy." Why did they respond in such a manner? Paul gave us the answer: "When He ascended on high, He . . . *gave gifts to men*" (Ephesians 4:8, emphasis added). He left them with special spiritual gifts that empowered them to carry on His work. Discovering these gifts brought "great joy" to each of them. When you discover your own gift, it will result in the same great joy.

As we have already acknowledged, these gifts are not natural abilities. There is a huge divide between a natural ability and a supernatural, sovereignly bestowed spiritual gift. An opera singer with natural and impeccable musical and vocal abilities might sing in a church service and not lead the people into a true worship experience nearly as much as someone who does not have the precise natural abilities of an operatic superstar but who does have a spiritual gift that God uses to build up His body.

Yes, God has given every believer a spiritual gift. No one is left out. Every single believer has one. It may not yet be recognized or exercised, but this special gift anointing is there inside each of us, waiting to be discovered. The Bible makes this plain, saying that "there are diversities of gifts, but the same Spirit. There are differences of ministries, but the same Lord. And there are diversities of activities, but it is the same God who works all in all. But the manifestation of the Spirit is given to each one for the profit of all" (1 Corinthians 12:4–7). These manifested gifts are given to each of us. You are so unique and valuable to God that He has given you a special gift with which to bless the entire body of Christ.

> You are so unique and valuable to God that He has given you a special gift with which to bless the entire body of Christ.

Importantly, while each of us has at least one gift, no one person has all the gifts. Paul made this clear, too, as he closed the twelfth chapter of 1 Corinthians: "Are all apostles? Are all prophets? Are all teachers? Are all workers of miracles? Do all have gifts of healings? Do all speak with tongues? Do all interpret?" (1 Corinthians 12:29–30). The answer was obvious—No! No one has all the gifts. But Paul finished the thought by saying we should "earnestly desire the best gifts. And yet I show you a more excellent way" (1 Corinthians 12:31). And with that word he launched into the thirteenth chapter of his epistle, revealing that love is the "more excellent way."

Every spiritual gift should be operated within the environment of the love of Christ. Paul made this point clear as well: "Though I speak with the tongues of men and of angels, but have not love, I have become sounding brass or a clanging cymbal. And though I have the gift of prophecy . . . and though I have all faith . . . but have not love, I am nothing" (1 Corinthians 13:1–2).

The twelfth, thirteenth, and fourteenth chapters of this first letter to the Corinthian believers contain Paul's dissertation on spiritual gifts. In chapter twelve Paul laid out the gifts. In chapter fourteen, he warned and pointed out how they are often perverted from their intended use. But in between, in chapter thirteen, he revealed that love is the measure, the standard—the "greatest of these is love" (1 Corinthians 13:13). This is like a Holy Spirit sandwich, and love is the filling. Love is the very oxygen in which the kingdom of God

> Love is the very oxygen in which the kingdom of God operates, and without love, we, like Paul, are nothing more than sounding brass or clanging cymbals.

operates, and without love, we, like Paul, are nothing more than sounding brass or clanging cymbals.

As we have noted previously, all believers—you, me, every single one of us—are likened to a body. We are, in fact, the visible body of Christ to the world today. While we are dependent upon the Holy Spirit for our spiritual life, we are interdependent upon one another as well. Like members of our own physical body, we must work together in love and unity to accomplish His will. This is why each of us is especially gifted for a unique purpose to function in the body of Christ.

We must forget the idea that the church is an organization. It was never primarily intended to be such. You are part of a living organism: the church, the body of Christ. My own physical body depends on the health and strength of every part of it. If one part ceases to function like it is designed to do, my whole body is affected. If my liver ceased functioning, I would not say, "Oh, I have lots of other organs. I am not going to worry about this one." Every part of my body is interdependent on every other part. And so it is with the body of Christ. We can't say of another believer, "We don't need her. Forget her—we're okay without her."

To this Paul said, "There should be no schism in the

body, but that the members should have the same care for one another. And if one member suffers, all the members suffer with it; or if one member is honored, all the members rejoice with it. Now you are the body of Christ, and members individually" (1 Corinthians 12:25–27). In the distribution and the functioning of the gifts, we are dependent upon the Holy Spirit. But in order to function as Christ intends, we are interdependent on each other.

God has given these gifts to us. They are not earned nor deserved. They are supernaturally bestowed by a sovereign Lord. Every believer has a gift. No believer has all the gifts. They are to be used for God's glory, for the uplifting and building up of the church, the body of Christ. And they are always to be exercised in an environment of love. They are designed "for the equipping of the saints for the work of the ministry, for the edifying of the body of Christ" (Ephesians 4:12).

These gifts, listed primarily in Paul's letters to the Corinthians, the Romans, and the Ephesians, are given with three distinct characteristics. There are *motivational* gifts designed to encourage the church. There are *miracle* gifts that prove the authenticity of the faith. And there are *ministry* gifts that seek to meet the needs of the entire body of believers. Remember, you have at least one. As we journey through the list of gifts in these next few chapters, see if you can discern which one(s) have been given to you, so that it might be said of us what was said of those early believers, that we, too, were characterized by "great joy."

21 THE GIFT LIST: MOTIVATIONAL GIFTS

*I*n Ephesians 4, Paul lays out the *motivational* gifts, some of which were specific to the early church's beginning and some of which continue to motivate believers in the family of faith. Paul presented this list with these words, "He Himself gave some to be apostles, some prophets, some evangelists, and some pastors and teachers" (Ephesians 4:11).

We'll begin our discussion with the spiritual gift of the apostle. Does anyone have this gift today? Some would say that in a very broad sense, we are all apostles. The word literally speaks of someone who is sent out with a commission from a higher authority, and Jesus issued a commission to every believer when He said, "As the Father has sent Me, I also send you" (John 20:21). But in a more specific biblical sense, no one today can claim this gift. One of the qualifications of an apostle was that he had to have seen the resurrected Lord Jesus personally with his own eyes. Paul addressed this, saying, "Am I not an apostle? Am I not free? Have I not seen Jesus Christ our Lord? Are you not my work in the Lord? If I am not an apostle to others, yet doubtless I am to you. For you are the seal of my apostleship in the Lord" (1 Corinthians 9:1–2).

The motivational gift of the apostle was a temporary gift given by Christ to help launch the church into the world. We know this because we read that the church was "built on the foundation of the apostles and prophets, Jesus Christ Himself being the chief cornerstone" (Ephesians 2:20). We do not have to be experts on architecture or building construction to know that in the building of a great structure, the foundation is laid first. The foundation of the church of the Lord Jesus Christ was completed long ago. It is done. We have been building upon that solid foundation for over two thousand years now. It would be an utter absurdity to construct a tall building and then, at the end, put a foundation on top of it. The foundation goes first. Two millennia ago, the apostles fulfilled their ministry. They were the foundation upon which the true

> The foundation of the church of the Lord Jesus Christ was completed long ago. It is done. We have been building upon that solid foundation for over two thousand years now.

church of Jesus Christ has been building throughout all these past centuries. The spiritual gift of the apostle was a temporary gifting and has long since passed.

The second of these motivational gifts is that of the prophets. A prophet was one who spoke not by illumination but by revelation from God. Remember, the believers in New Testament days did not have what we possess today, that being the final revelation to man from God that we call the Bible. The people we read about in the Gospels, in the book of Acts, and in all of Paul's epistles never saw a New Testament. The books it contains had not yet been written. So how could these early churches know God's will and way for them? God gifted certain men throughout Bible days to speak His Word.

There is a difference between a prophet and a priest. A priest speaks to God about men. A prophet spoke God's Word to men by divine revelation. The prophets, along with the apostles, were part of the foundation of the church (Ephesians 2:20). Consequently, this gift, like that of the apostle, was temporary.

The prophets spoke to people from direct and divine revelation from God. The mark of a true prophet was not that they were accurate 50 percent of the time, but that what they said always did or will come true in the end.

Today, the church does not need prophets in the purest biblical sense of the word. Why? We have the final and complete revelation from God to man in the words of the Bible. In fact, the Bible closes with the warning of a curse on anyone who adds to or takes away from God's Word (Revelation 22:19). Jude reminded us that we are to "contend earnestly for the faith which was *once for all* delivered to the saints" (Jude 3, emphasis added). We don't get new revelation today. We have the final and complete revelation from God in our Bibles. We do not need revelation; we need illumination. Every believer can find this illumination of the sacred text through the Holy Spirit, our teacher.

> We do not need revelation; we need illumination. Every believer can find this illumination of the sacred text through the Holy Spirit, our teacher.

While the first two motivational gifts, those of the apostles and the prophets, were temporary in their distribution, the remainder of the motivational gifts are permanent and continue in every generation. Paul spoke next of the gift of the evangelist. The evangelist is especially gifted as a bearer of the good news of the gospel. While we all should be doing the *work* of the evangelist (sharing the gospel), not all of us are gifted with the spiritual gift to do the *ministry* of evangelism. Those gifted as evangelists have been building on the foundation the apostles and prophets laid by reaching the lost. God still gives certain people this gift today. In the past generation, we can point specifically to Billy Graham, among thousands of others across the world, who had this special spiritual gift to call people to Christ. God fills the evangelist's heart with a fervent gift for the lost and a unique ability to call them to Christ.

Paul continued with the motivational gift of the "pastor-teacher." This is not referring to two different people but one. The gifted pastor is one who not only leads a flock but teaches them the deep truths of Scripture as well. Paul links the pastors and teachers together. This gift is bestowed upon those whom God calls to be pastoring teachers and teaching pastors. True pastors are given the heart of a shepherd and given charge and responsibility over the souls of God's children. They are not just pleasant people with natural abilities to speak in soft voices and smile a lot. They are the guardians, the custodians, the protectors, the leaders of God's people. Scripture refers to a pastor as the "under shepherd" of the Great Shepherd Himself, the Lord Jesus Christ (1 Peter 5:1–4).

All of these motivational gifts come together to produce

love and motivate unity in the church. The apostles and prophets laid the foundation. The evangelists come to win the lost and place them in the buildings we call the church. The pastor-teachers then instruct in doctrine and righteousness to build up the body of Christ. These are the motivational gifts God has given the church.

22 THE GIFT LIST: MINISTRY GIFTS

*W*hile the Lord gifts some of us with motivational gifts to get the church going, the ministry gifts God gives to those in His body enable the church to build up in the faith those whom He has called unto Himself. These ministry gifts are listed primarily in Paul's letter to the Romans in chapter twelve and in his discourse on the gifts of the Spirit in the twelfth chapter of his first Corinthian epistle. They are the gifts of prophecy, help, teaching, exhortation, giving, administration, mercy, knowledge, wisdom, faith, and discernment. It is in this grouping of ministry gifts (and not in the motivational or miracle gifts) that most believers find their spiritual gift and put it to use in Christ's kingdom.

The Bible teaches that God gifts a certain and specific ministry gift of prophecy to particular members of His body. The gift of prophecy is to be differentiated from the gift of the prophet, which we have seen was temporary and among the motivational gifts. The gift of prophecy is not reserved for pastors or teachers but distributed to various members in Christ's family. This gift is often perverted by those who announce they have received some type of extrabiblical revelation for someone or something. The spiritual gift of prophecy is something else entirely.

The Bible is our all-sufficient guide. Everything we need to know is found within its pages between Genesis 1:1 and Revelation 22:21. All Scripture points to Jesus. A key to understanding the spiritual gift of prophecy is found in Revelation 19:10: "The testimony of Jesus is the spirit of prophecy." This gift enables one to spiritually proclaim the living Word of God from the written Word of God with clarity and conviction. When someone has the gift of prophecy, they will perform it in such a way that it brings encouragement, edification, and comfort to the people (1 Corinthians 14:3).

> When someone has the gift of prophecy, they will perform it in such a way that it brings encouragement, edification, and comfort to the people.

Next is what the Bible refers to as the gift of "helps" (1 Corinthians 12:28). God gifts certain people with the supernatural ability to be present when any and all types of help are needed, and they provide that help with joyful hearts. We have all known people with this special gift. Outlets for exercising this gift are limitless within and without the church.

Closely associated with the gift of helps is the gift of hospitality. Paul mentions that some are "given to hospitality" (Romans 12:13). The word *hospitality* is derived from the word *hospital* or *hospice*. Those who possess this spiritual gift are a haven to those in distress or need. An open house, a place at the table, and a warm welcome are characteristic of those with gifts of helps and hospitality.

There is also the ministry gift of teaching. Paul admonished, "Having then gifts differing according to the grace that is given to us, let us use them . . . he who teaches, in teaching" (Romans 12:6–7). There are many teachers today, but those possessing the spiritual gift of teaching have the supernatural giftedness to make plain the message of a text of Scripture and how to properly apply it to life situations. This is what distinguishes a teacher from one with the gift of teaching. Teachers can present facts, but we need someone with this special supernatural gift to make the facts concise and clear and to help us put them into practice at the point of our need. Most of us know men and women who exercise this amazing spiritual gift.

Another ministry gift is what the Bible calls the gift of

exhortation (Romans 12:8). Someone who has been given the gift of exhortation will be an encourager of the highest order. This gift is the supernatural ability to stand alongside those who are hurting with words of help and hope, to bring strength to those who are growing weak and about to give up or give in, to lift up those who are sinking in their faith, and to bring comfort and assurance to those who are doubting. Throughout the book of Acts, we find Paul exercising this spiritual gift. On his return to Antioch, he was "strengthening the souls of the disciples, exhorting them to continue in the faith" (Acts 14:22). Paul's farewell speech, made on his final visit to Ephesus and perhaps given through tears, was one of endearing exhortation and well worth reading (Acts 20:17–35). We all need men and women with the gift of exhortation in our circle of influence.

> Someone who has been given the gift of exhortation will be an encourager of the highest order.

Next on the list comes the gift of giving. We all have the biblical responsibility to tithe our income. I have never understood why those of us who live under grace think we should give less than those in the old dispensation who were living under the law. But while every believer is to give liberally to the work of Christ, this gift is a special enablement to give above and beyond what is required of him or her. It brings tremendous joy to the giver and great blessing to the church. Most of us can readily point to someone who has this gift of giving. In my own experience, I have known far more people with this gift who had little in the way of worldly wealth than I have those who possessed much. Those with this spiritual gift give with no ulterior motive and out of grateful hearts "not grudgingly or of necessity" (2 Corinthians 9:7).

Next, some have been given the ministry gift of administration with unique abilities to lead others. This gift is mentioned in Romans 12:8 as one who "leads, with diligence." Christian leadership is never to be exercised in an environment that is dictatorial, demagogic, or even dogmatic. It should be exercised by one who is "full of the Holy Spirit and wisdom" (Acts 6:3), who also reflects the qualities required for deacon leadership. The one who has the spiritual gift of leadership will be one who plans for the future and does so as a servant leader.

Romans 12:8 also mentions the ministry gift of mercy. While every believer should lean more on the side of mercy than judgment, this special gift of the Holy Spirit is manifested by men and women who have a supernatural compassion for a suffering brother or sister in Christ who is in crisis or in need. Those with this gift do not just care for others but openly share with them at the point of their need. Possessing this gift or observing others who have it should be a reminder that if we are going to

> If we are going to make a mistake, we should make it on the side of mercy and not judgment.

make a mistake, we should make it on the side of mercy and not judgment.

God also supernaturally gifts some believers with the gifts of knowledge and wisdom. Knowledge is the accumulation of facts, while wisdom is the supernatural ability to discern those facts with godly wisdom. These ministry gifts are found in 1 Corinthians 12:8. This gift of wisdom is the ability to apply knowledge to certain challenging and difficult situations. The gift of wisdom never results in confusion or conflict but is exercised with gentleness, mercy, and peace, according to James 3:15–18.

God also supernaturally gifts certain men and women with the gift of faith (1 Corinthians 12:9). When common sense is saying a situation is hopeless, God gifts some people with the uncommon sense (faith) to believe that He can still make the impossible possible. Those with this spiritual gift have the capacity to see something that God desires done and, in the face of seemingly insurmountable

> When common sense is saying a situation is hopeless, God gifts some people with the uncommon sense (faith) to believe that He can still make the impossible possible.

obstacles, maintain a confidence that His will and way will be accomplished. We need to look no further than Stephen for an example of the gift of faith (Acts 6:8–20).

Finally, there is the ministry gift of discernment (1 Corinthians 12:10). This is the God-given spiritual gift enabling us to discern between the spirit of truth and the spirit of error. Perhaps one of the church's greatest needs today is men and women who not only possess this gift but use it in days of theological confusion. A person possessing this gift can read a book or listen to a sermon or teaching and immediately detect error. They can sit in a worship service and detect whether there is simply a superficial emotion taking place or a supernatural emotion firmly fixed in biblical truth. We should be especially grateful for individuals who have and use this gift.

God's church is a living organism administered through spiritual gifts and not mere human abilities. We've looked at the motivational gifts and ministry gifts He bestows on us to accomplish this task. Now let's look at the miracle gifts that defy human explanation.

23 THE GIFT LIST: MIRACLE GIFTS

*W*hile the church operates today through the *motivational* gifts like those of the evangelist and the pastor-teacher along with the *ministry* gifts, such as mercy or helps or wisdom or faith, too often it is the *miracle* gifts that some seem to push onto center stage. Paul lists these miracle gifts (also called signs) in 1 Corinthians 12:8–10, including the "gifts of healings . . . the working of miracles . . . [and] different kinds of tongues."

The Bible speaks of those who have the special spiritual gift of working miracles. A miracle takes place when the laws of nature are superseded by unexplained supernatural power. God is not bound by any cell He has ever created nor by any law of nature. After all, He put them all in place. We read of miracles frequently in the life of Christ. He walked on water, fed thousands of people with a few loaves and fish, gave sight to the blind, raised the dead to life again, and brought healing to men and women with all kinds of afflictions and diseases. It is no wonder we call Him the miracle worker.

But the Bible declares that these gifts of miracles were given to some in the early church as well. Indeed, we see miracle after miracle on almost every page of the book of Acts as it chronicles the exploits of first-century believers. Paul reminded the church in Corinth that "the signs of an apostle were accomplished among you with all perseverance, in signs and wonders and mighty deeds" (2 Corinthians 12:12). And to the Romans he declared that the authentic mark of his apostolic calling was the working of miracles Christ performed through him, validating the gospel message by "mighty signs and wonders, by the power of the Spirit of God" (Romans 15:19).

Does anyone have this spiritual gift of miracles today, manifested by "signs and wonders"? Make no mistake—God is still in the miracle-working business. There is no doubt about that. But the special gift of miracles can be operated at will by those who have it just like it was done in the Gospels and Acts. A person with this gift today would be able, through a word or a command, to suspend the laws of nature in order to operate in this

> Make no mistake—
> God is still in the
> miracle-working
> business.

gift. He or she would be able to do it at will too—anytime, anyplace. Are miracles still possible today? Absolutely. But there is a difference between a sovereign God acting of His own will to bring about a miracle and someone who might claim to have the spiritual gift of working miracles.

Paul adds another gift to these miracle gifts: the gift of healing. This spiritual gift of healing enables the recipient to suspend the laws of nature to bring about an immediate restoration of health to an individual. Anyone who has ever read the Gospels has seen that Jesus "went about all the cities and villages . . . healing every sickness and every disease among the people" (Matthew 9:35). There is not one time where we read that any sick man, woman, boy, or girl who came to Him was not healed and restored to health. Peter also had this gift of healing. We see him healing a lame man (Acts 3:1–9) and a paralytic (Acts 9:32–34) with a spoken word. Later he raised Dorcas from the dead (Acts 9:36–41).

But does anyone have this gift today, enabling them to heal people at will with a word or command? If so, why are they not going from room to room in the hospitals? Do I believe that God is still in the healing business? Yes. I have seen people miraculously healed. But the gift of healing is a different thing. One of the most famous faith healers of all time once told me he did not think he had the spiritual gift of healing but the gift of faith to believe for supernatural healings.

Finally, we come to the gift of tongues, listed as a miracle gift given to the church. The Bible records that at Pentecost, they "began to speak with other tongues, as the Spirit gave them utterance" (Acts 2:4). These tongues were known languages. The real miracle of Pentecost was in the hearing: "Everyone heard them speak in his own language" (Acts 2:6).

What was happening at Pentecost? Jews had gathered in Jerusalem from a multitude of different countries all over the Mediterranean world. These people spoke many different languages. God gave Peter the ability to speak in such a way that everyone under the sound of his voice actually heard what he was saying in their own language. But that is not all—they heard him, not just in their own language but in their own unique dialect. The gift of tongues in Acts 2 was not an incoherent babbling. It was linguistic. It was miraculous and got the attention of the vast crowd. Then Peter preached the gospel, and three thousand men and women came to faith in Christ. The church was born in a day.

While the "tongues" we read about when the gospel

came to the Jews in Acts 2 and to the Gentiles in Acts 10 were known languages, the speaker there was supernaturally empowered to translate the gospel to different language groups. The tongues we read about in 1 Corinthians 12–14 are of a different nature. There are those in this age of grace who believe this Corinthian gift of tongues to be an ecstatic utterance. In some cases, the gift is referred to as a prayer language. Regardless, it is listed among the least of the gifts, and Paul stated, "Though I speak with the tongues of men and of angels, but have not love, I have become sounding brass or a clanging cymbal" (1 Corinthians 13:1).

If tongues, these ecstatic utterances, were as important for our Christian growth and Spirit-filled living as some today make them out to be, surely Paul would have had more to say regarding them. He addressed them in 1 Corinthians 14 as a problem that often brought about confusion. While there have always been and remain today great numbers of true and sincere believers who speak in what might be refered to as "the tongues of men and angels" this gift, when genuine, will always be operated within biblical parameters. After his lengthy discourse there, Paul wrote the Roman letter, the great theological discourse, and never mentioned this gift of tongues. After he wrote to the Corinthians he also wrote to the

Ephesians, the Philippians, the Colossians, to Timothy and to Titus and to Philemon, and not once in any of these letters is found one word about the importance of speaking in tongues or the other miracle gifts. Why? Perhaps the key is found in 1 Corinthians 13:8–10, 13: "Love never fails. But . . . whether there are tongues, they will cease . . . when that which is perfect has come, then that which is in part will be done away. . . . Now abide faith, hope, love, these three; but the greatest of these is love."

As we read the Bible, we find that God introduced every new dispensation with signs and wonders and miracles that were never repeated again. In the first dispensation when God spoke into existence all the created order in the early verses of Genesis, He did so with signs and wonders and miracles. He created everything out of nothing with a spoken word. He spoke, and it was so. We call this "fiat creation." Not since those early verses of Scripture are we told that God created another single atom out of nothing. Consider the dispensation of the law. That, too, was ushered in by signs and wonders and miracles that have not been duplicated since the days of Moses. The

> As we read the Bible, we find that God introduced every new dispensation with signs and wonders and miracles that were never repeated again.

parting of the Red Sea, the cloud by day and the pillar of fire by night that led the Israelites, and the manna that fell from heaven each day to sustain them in the wilderness are miracles that have never been repeated. And so it was with the age of grace, the church age. It, too, was ushered in with the amazing signs and wonders we read about in the book of Acts.

The church of Jesus Christ is a living organism, not just another human organization. And God, through the Holy Spirit, has gifted each member with special supernatural spiritual gifts for the building up of the body of Christ in order to produce love and unity. Now that we have examined these gifts, let's keep reading and make the wonderful discovery of how we can recognize our own gifts which God has freely given to each of us. And then, let us begin to use them for His glory.

24 OPEN YOUR GIFT

*W*e've all been the recipients of beautifully wrapped gifts at Christmas, birthdays, and other special occasions. Can you imagine someone giving you a gift that you never take the time to open? What good is a gift if it is left untouched and unopened? God has given every believer a gift from the Holy Spirit, but tragically, many of those gifts are unacknowledged, unopened, and unused. It is time to recognize your own special gift, open it, and use it for God's glory and for the benefit of His church here on earth.

These gifts from God are uniquely given to each and every believer (Ephesians 4:7). They are not given because of any natural ability we may or may not possess. Neither are they given for merit as if they were earned or deserved. These spiritual gifts are given to every believer at their moment of conversion. Since these are gifts of God, they are not to be *sought*. However, Paul does say we should "earnestly desire the best gifts" (1 Corinthians 12:31). One of the issues in Corinth was that the believers were maximizing the minor gifts and minimizing the major ones. We don't seek gifts; they are given to us by Someone who loves us.

Spiritual gifts are not to be *sought*, and they cannot be *caught*. We do not receive a spiritual gift by staying close to others who have them, hoping they might rub off on us. Neither can they be *taught*. They are just what they are: gifts. From time to time, we might be confronted by well-meaning believers who try to teach us how to use a particular gift, usually tongues. My experience is that those who attempt to teach others how to use those gifts seldom teach how to use the gifts of faith or mercy.

We might add that spiritual gifts cannot be *bought* either. You can't buy a gift. When someone gives you a gift and you try to reciprocate with cash, it is no longer a gift. It becomes something you bought. You can do this at the store. Finally, we would note that the gifts should not be *fought*. Never fight against what God has gifted you. He has your highest benefit and blessing in mind.

> Spiritual gifts are not to be *sought*, and they cannot be *caught*.

These sovereignly bestowed gifts given by Christ are grace gifts—they are unmerited. There is not a single verse, not even in the most detailed explanation of spiritual gifts found in 1 Corinthians 12–14, that talks about the fullness of the Holy Spirit. The exercise of any of these gifts is not the proof of the fullness of the Holy Spirit in your life. They are given for equipping, not evidence. Love, the "more excellent way" (1 Corinthians 12:31), is one evidence of His fullness in our lives.

How can you know you have a certain gift of the Holy Spirit? First, you will know by your own personal inclination. You will love to use it. Those with the gifts of mercy or helps find their greatest joy in being Christ's hand extended to someone in need. Those with the spiritual gift of giving love sharing what they have with others in expanding the work of the kingdom. Those who have the gift of the pastor could never imagine doing anything else. Leading and feeding the church of the Lord Jesus is where they find purpose and fulfillment. Add to the element of personal inclination the fact that spiritually mindful people in the church will recognize gifts in other people, and the church will use them.

Once you discover your own spiritual gift, it will be productive. It will draw you into service. Anyone who discovers and uses their spiritual gift will be immersed in the service of Jesus. It will produce unity in the body.

And it will produce a new or strengthened environment of love. The Bible says, "I show you a more excellent way" (1 Corinthians 12:31). Paul then continued into the well-known thirteenth chapter, showing that more excellent way to be love.

> Though I speak with the tongues of men and of angels, but have not love, I have become sounding brass or a clanging cymbal. And though I have the gift of prophecy, and understand all mysteries and all knowledge, and though I have all faith, so that I could remove mountains, but have not love, I am nothing. And though I bestow all my goods to feed the poor, and though I give my body to be burned, but have not love, it profits me nothing. (1 Corinthians 13:1–3)

These are strong words. Yet, love is the environment in which we use our gifts best for God's glory. Without love, we, too, are nothing.

We should be grateful that these spiritual gifts are given by an all-knowing God. Who of us would have chosen and gifted a motley group of rough Galilean fishermen and others to change the world? These are gifts from God Himself. Our churches and seminaries are not factories;

they should be refineries where believers can sharpen and refine their God-given callings and giftedness for use. The question in God's kingdom is never "Are we qualified?" It should be "Are we called and gifted?"

Our God-given gifts are "for the equipping of the saints for the work of ministry, for the edifying of the body of Christ, till we all come to the unity of the faith and of the knowledge of the Son of God" (Ephesians 4:12–13). These gifts of the Holy Spirit are personal, purposeful, and profitable when they are recognized and used for His glory.

You have a gift. Identify it. Open it. Use it. You will love what God has gifted you to do. And the church will recognize it and be blessed by it. Go ahead—unwrap it.

25 MAKING THE MOST OF YOUR GIFT

*W*e have looked long and hard at the gifts of the Holy Spirit in the preceding chapters. What is the end game? When recognized and used, these gifts of grace produce maturity in the life of the believer. Your spiritual gift should produce maturity in *character*. How long are we to keep going? How long are we to continue the "equipping of the saints for the work of ministry, for the edifying of the body of Christ"? *Until.* But until when? Until "we all come to the unity of the faith and of the knowledge of the Son of God, to a perfect man, to the measure of the stature of the fullness of Christ" (Ephesians 4:12–13).

We certainly have a ways to go. When does this come to an end? Not until Jesus Christ returns for us. There will come a day when the body of Christ, the church, will be fully developed, fully grown, fully mature. It is not that way now. But one day the last person that will make up this fully mature body will be saved, and Jesus will come again. One day the body of Christ will be complete, and we will become the bride of Christ. There is a real sense that without you, the body will never be complete. You are an important part of His body, and your gifts are given to help build it up. But one day out there on God's calendar of eternity, there will be "unity of the faith and of the knowledge of the Son of God." We are vital, important members of His body, each uniquely gifted to do our part until we come to that day. Recognizing and using our spiritual gifts will produce maturity in character as we become more like Christ.

> Recognizing and using our spiritual gifts will produce maturity in character as we become more like Christ.

The gifts are also given to produce maturity in our *conduct.* We all began this Christian experience as babies, just "born again" by the Spirit. We started like little children and not mature adults. Then we grew and matured in the faith. It is a tragedy that some of us remain immature children, even after years or decades of claiming to know Christ. Growing and maturing in the faith is a process. While Scripture exhorts us to be childlike in our faith, it abhors our being childish. The biblical admonition is "that we should no longer be children, tossed to and fro and carried about with every wind of doctrine" (Ephesians 4:14).

Children are fragile. They are easily tossed to and fro. Children are often stubborn, always wanting their own way. They have difficulty learning hard lessons. They get easily upset. If you don't believe that, don't give one their bottle at the right time, and see what happens. Children are given to quarreling at the least offense. They have a tendency to play when big things are happening.

Nothing is more tragic in the life of a believer than to remain a child in the faith. The recognition of spiritual gifts and their use in God's kingdom can produce maturity, not just in character but in conduct for the believer.

A man or woman being filled with God's Spirit and aware of the spiritual gifts will also show maturity in *conversation*. They will speak the truth in love (Ephesians 4:15). It is one thing to speak the truth but quite another to speak it in love. Some speak the truth but not in the environment of love. Others speak in love but sacrifice the hard truth. There is no Christian maturity without the element of truth. Mere friendliness and kindness do not constitute Christianity if truth is

> It is one thing to speak the truth but quite another to speak it in love.

sacrificed in the process. On the other hand, just because someone speaks the truth does not mean they are mature. Truth in love is the key to Christian maturity.

Real truth should always produce love. We are called to speak the truth in order to win the lost—not simply to show them we are intellectually or spiritually superior. How do we do that? With love. We need to look upon people with the eyes of Christ who saw them as "sheep without a shepherd" and had compassion for them (Matthew 9:36). Speaking the truth and doing so in love is a mark of maturity that emits from a life being controlled by God's Spirit.

When realized and recognized, Christ's gifts to us also produce maturity in *cooperation*. Ephesians 4:16 states that Christ as the head desires His whole body to be "joined and knit together." My own body parts are designed in such a way to meet each other's needs in cooperation. Consider my hip joint. The joint is like a cup, and into that cup perfectly fits a smooth ball on the end of my femur. The joint works easily and in harmony. This is exactly God's intent for His church. Every part of the body is intended to work together in cooperation and harmony.

What if the body had no joints? What if the arm extended into the hand without a wrist joint? There would be friction and dysfunction. We all need each other in

Christ's body. Growth in maturity is not just to perform your own spiritual gifts but to accept the gifts and ministries of others. We need each other, and a mark of Christian maturity is acknowledging this fact so that Christ's body works in harmony and cooperation to present to the world a picture of Jesus.

The principle of love is woven repeatedly throughout the biblical passages on the gifts of the Spirit. Love is the key. "Now abide faith, hope, love, these three; but the greatest of these is love" (1 Corinthians 13:13). Discover your spiritual gift. Use it for the good of Christ's church, His body. And make sure you live your life and use your spiritual gift in the environment of His divine love.

26 THE BATTLE LINES ARE DRAWN

*T*he Christian life is not intended to be lived on flowery beds of ease. When we are being filled with God's Spirit, we can expect to meet the devil head-on. In fact, if we are *not* meeting him head-on, it might be that we are going in the same direction as him. The battle lines have been drawn for us in what the Bible calls the "works of the flesh" versus the "fruit of the Spirit." They war against one another, vie for our attention, and are contrary to one another.

Paul laid this out clearly in Galatians 5.

Walk in the Spirit, and you shall not fulfill the lust of the flesh. For the flesh lusts against the Spirit, and the Spirit against the flesh; and these are contrary to one another, so that you do not do the things that you wish. But if you are led by the Spirit, you are not under the law.

Now the works of the flesh are evident, which are:

adultery, fornication, uncleanness, lewdness, idolatry, sorcery, hatred, contentions, jealousies, outbursts of wrath, selfish ambitions, dissensions, heresies, envy, murders, drunkenness, revelries, and the like; of which I tell you beforehand, just as I also told you in time past, that those who practice such things will not inherit the kingdom of God.

But the fruit of the Spirit is love, joy, peace, long-suffering, kindness, goodness, faithfulness, gentleness, self-control. Against such there is no law. And those who are Christ's have crucified the flesh with its passions and desires. If we live in the Spirit, let us also walk in the Spirit. Let us not become conceited, provoking one another, envying one another. (Galatians 5:16–26)

The Bible refers to that period of time between our conversion to Christ and the time we go to heaven as the walk of the believer. According to Galatians 5:16, we are expected to walk in the Spirit. If we *live* in the Spirit, then verse 25 says we should also *walk* in the Spirit. We have all known those who walked the Christian life for decades with seemingly little victory, while others journeyed only a short distance in the Christian walk before they died, yet their lives were manifested in joy and victory. For

> It is not *how far* we walk but *how* we walk this Christian journey that makes the difference.

many Christians, the walk takes them through dark valleys with little light. Others seem to stumble over obstacles all along the way. Still others keep running into dead ends or detours. It is not *how far* we walk but *how* we walk this Christian journey that makes the difference.

Throughout our married life, my wife Susie and I have maintained a discipline of daily physical exercise. We enjoy early morning walks together, especially in the fall and spring. Something about a walk clears our minds of the clutter that accumulates with all the things that come our way. It provides an uninterrupted opportunity to talk with each other about the deeper things of our hearts and brings an intimacy that is not just helpful but essential in our lives.

Walking in the Spirit does the same thing for our spiritual lives. To walk in the Spirit means that we are living our lives with a mindset of focus on the Lord and His commandments and blessings. The Lord desires intimacy and longs for us to live in a relationship of intimacy with Him as Father and child.

Jesus often spoke about this "walk" of the believer. He

said, "I am the light of the world. He who follows Me shall not walk in darkness, but have the light of life" (John 8:12). On another occasion He told the disciples, "A little while longer the light is with you. Walk while you have the light, lest darkness overtake you; he who walks in darkness does not know where he is going" (John 12:35). When we walk in the Spirit, not only does it help us to "not fulfill the lust of the flesh" but it brings direction to our lives. It lights our way.

Paul spoke of "walking in the Spirit" in almost every letter he wrote. In 2 Corinthians 5:7, he challenged us to "walk by faith, not by sight." In Colossians 2:6, he reminded us, "As you therefore have received Christ Jesus the Lord, so walk in Him." How did you receive Christ Jesus the Lord? Was it by works, by being good enough, by all the human effort you could muster? No. The Bible is clear: we are saved by faith and faith alone.

If faith is good enough to save us, it is also good enough to live and walk by in our Christian life. This is a walk of faith, not of feeling or sight. Further, God has His own way of honoring those who honor Him by walking in faith, because when we do, "there is therefore now no condemnation to those who are in Christ Jesus, who do not walk according to the flesh, but according to the

Spirit" (Romans 8:1). There is no condemnation or judgment for those who understand the battle lines and choose the right side.

God never intended the Christian walk to be one of discouragement, darkness, or defeat. Certainly as we walk this journey, there will be problems that hinder our progress. But there are also proofs that highlight our walk of faith. It is time to pick sides. The battle lines are drawn. Let's turn the page and look at some of the problems that Satan puts in our way to hinder our walk in the Spirit.

27 A WALK IN THE SPIRIT: PROBLEMS THAT HINDER

*A*ll who have walked this Christian path have had their own experiences along the way when, as Paul said, they did not do the things they wished they had done. Why is that? Because this war within us between the flesh and the spirit never ends. "The flesh lusts against the Spirit, and the Spirit against the flesh" (Galatians 5:17). The battle lines are drawn within our own hearts between the works of the flesh and the fruit of the Spirit. Those who lead armies into battle gather all they can know about the enemy's strategy before they engage in battle. Knowing this, Paul laid out some military intelligence for us so we could see what might hinder us in our march to victory in the Christian life.

Many lose the battle because of *desires that are misdirected*. These misdirected desires consist of adultery, fornication, uncleanness, and lewdness (Galatians 5:19). Adultery and fornication speak for themselves. They are the height of immorality. Uncleanness deals more in the realm of our thought life; the lusts of the flesh that are conjured up in our minds. Lewdness expresses the idea of one who is so far gone in lust and forbidden, ungodly desires that he or she no longer cares what people say or think of them. Sins that once slithered through back alleys now parade proudly down Main Street, where virginity and purity seem to be so out of date.

Why did God say, "You shall not commit adultery" (Exodus 20:14)? Was it just to rob you of some type of satisfaction? Not at all. God gave this commandment because He loves us and seeks our highest good. He knew that if we chose to live in adultery, fornication, uncleanness, or lewdness, we would constantly be looking over our shoulders, hoping we would not be found out. One lie would have to cover another lie to hide our transgressions. God gave us commandments so we could live happy and fruitful lives. A train is much freer to operate as intended when it is running on the tracks and not heading out into some open field.

> God gave us commandments so we could live happy and fruitful lives.

There are other hindrances to our walk of faith in the Spirit. These are *misguided devotions*. The Bible lists them as idolatry and sorcery (Galatians 5:20). The word *sorcery* comes from the same word from which we derive the word *pharmacy*. It had to do with the use of drugs even in Paul's day. Idolatry is the worship of gods that human hands have made. In our sophisticated, modern, Western lifestyle, we may not be bowing down to some carved idol or wringing the head of a scrawny chicken and letting its blood flow over a grotesque mud idol, but idolatry remains a major problem hindering the Christian walk. We have our own misguided devotions. We bow down every day to the gods of this world that fill our own lives—a hobby, a job, perhaps a person we've allowed to become the object of our worship. Our personal idols are those things that demand our attention and devotion and that occupy our thoughts.

Why do you think God commanded us, saying, "You shall have no other gods before Me" (Exodus 20:3)? Is it because He is egotistical? No. He knew that the only way we would ever find true happiness was if we crowned Him the Lord of our lives and walked in His Spirit.

Another type of hindrance the devil sets up to interfere with our walk of victory is the *mismanaged disposition*. These dispositions are listed in Galatians 5:20–21. Among them are hatred and contentions. These describe someone who is filled with the spirit of strife, who is characteristically hostile toward other people. It is the exact opposite of the Christian virtue of love. Jealousy is next on the list. It is the desire to have what someone else has and enjoys. The list continues with such mismanaged dispositions as "outbursts of wrath, selfish ambitions, dissensions, heresies, envy, murders, drunkenness, revelries, and the like." How prone we often are to be characterized by some of these.

There is a war going on within us every day. The flesh fights against the Spirit in these three primary manners: misdirected desires, misguided devotions, and mismanaged dispositions. But after drawing the battle lines for us and cautioning us about the problems that hinder our walk with the Spirit, Paul drew a clarifying contrast. He provided a list of the fruit of the Spirit that should serve as proofs that highlight the life of every believer who walks according to the Spirit and not according to the flesh.

28 A WALK IN THE SPIRIT: PROOFS THAT HIGHLIGHT

*A*s we previously noted, when we are filled with God's Spirit, all of life is about relationships. There are three types of relationships in life: outward relationships with others in the home, office, social arena, or wherever; the inward relationship with ourselves, sometimes called self-worth or self-respect; and the upward relationship with God. We will never be properly related to each other until we are properly related to ourselves, and this will not take place until we find our self-worth in Christ by being properly related to Him through faith.

After revealing the works of the flesh that we discussed in the previous chapter, the apostle Paul moved on to highlight the fruit of the Spirit. In the words of Scripture, "The fruit of the Spirit is love, joy, peace, longsuffering, kindness, goodness, faithfulness, gentleness, self-control" (Galatians 5:22–23).

At first glance, there appears to be a grammatical error

here. Shouldn't it say "the fruits" of the Spirit instead of the singular "fruit" of the Spirit? After all, the text has just revealed the "works" of the flesh. But there is no error. The works of the flesh consist of a long list of separate acts that we are prone to commit. Hence, the plural form, "works." But the "fruit of the Spirit" is singular because it is the out-cropping of one life within. The fruit is *who we are*, while the works are what we do. The fruit is not produced by us but by the Holy Spirit within us. "Fruit" is singular because it indicates a cluster of grapes with nine distinct attributes all issuing out of love. The fruit of the Spirit is love! This fruit Paul mentioned is in three clusters, all of which issue out of love. Once again, as we observed with the gifts of the Spirit, love is the evidence of Spirit-filled fruit bearing in our lives.

> Love is the evidence of Spirit-filled fruit bearing in our lives.

This fruit is evidenced by love, joy, and peace. How will we recognize this fruit in others? *It will be obvious on their countenance.* Some individuals seem to have love, joy, and peace written on their faces. The word translated as *love* here is *agape*—God's love, the highest level of self-less and sacrificial love that always seeks another's highest good. It is no coincidence that love is listed first on the list of this cluster of nine fruits. It is the fountain of all others. Everything good issues out of the love of God.

Next comes joy. This is the inner joy that Christ brings and that reveals itself through our countenance to others. This is the very joy Jesus spoke about on the night before He was crucified: "These things I have spoken to you, that My joy may remain in you, and that your joy may be full" (John 15:11).

Peace completes this triad of fruit evidencing our relationship with God. An inner peace is God's special gift to believers. Again, He spoke of this the night before He died, saying, "Peace I leave with you, My peace I give to you; not as the world gives do I give to you. Let not your heart be troubled, neither let it be afraid" (John 14:27). When we are abiding in God's Spirit daily, it will be written on our faces. God's love, joy, and peace will be obvious in our countenance. We cannot manufacture these in and of ourselves. Love, joy, and peace are the by-products of a life abiding in Christ.

We find the outward proof of our relationship with God in the next cluster of fruit—long-suffering, kindness, and goodness. These traits reveal for all to see *conduct that is orderly. Long-suffering* is often translated as *patience.* It is a compound word in Greek which can be expressed

> Love's greatest triumph is not always in what love does, but in what love refrains from doing.

as "far from anger." This display of our conduct issues from within and cannot be worked up on our part. In our fast-paced, self-seeking world, patience seldom seems to be in high supply. Love's greatest triumph is not always in what love does, but in what love refrains from doing.

In our relationships with others, the conduct of people abiding in Christ is also characterized by kindness. Because God shows "the exceeding riches of His grace in His kindness toward us in Christ Jesus" (Ephesians 2:7), we are to pass this kindness on to others. It is the result of walking in the Spirit.

Paul next introduces the fruit called "goodness." Jesus "went about doing good" (Acts 10:38). A genuine sense of goodness emanates from those who abide in Christ. In our relationships, we will be patient, kind, and good to others around us. Those with whom we come into contact will know our goodness by who we are, not only by what we do. Our conduct, like our countenance, is the expression of the One who lives in us.

Finally, in our relationship with ourselves, the fruit will manifest a *character that is obedient*. We will be characterized by faithfulness, gentleness, and self-control. What could be better said of you or me than that we were faithful to God, to ourselves, and to others? There is something inherent about a life of faithfulness that strengthens our sense of self-worth.

The next fruit issuing out of our life in Christ and our walk in the Spirit is gentleness. This is the same word translated as *meek* in Matthew 5:5. On the surface it sounds a bit weak, but it is one of the strongest character traits that exists. We can picture meekness as a stallion that has been domesticated and brought under the control of its owner. In cowboy jargon, it has been broken. This once bucking bronco now has a tender gentleness about it. This is power on a leash, and it is the natural outflow of the Holy Spirit within us.

Finally, we come to the last piece of fruit in this spiritual cluster—self-control. Who among us could not use a little more of this? But self-control does not come by the outworking of mere fleshly energy and effort. Like all the fruit, it is the result of the outcropping of the Holy Spirit living within us. When we come to know Christ as our personal Savior, the Father sends the Holy Spirit not only to seal us, to indwell us, and to fill us, but also to produce fruit through us in all three of our relationship types:

upward with God, outward with others, and inward with ourselves.

Now is a good time to ask ourselves a few questions: *What about my countenance? Do others see the love, peace, and joy of the Spirit in me? What about my conduct? Would anyone say they see patience, goodness, and kindness in me? And what about my character? Do I exhibit faithfulness, gentleness, or self-control?* Remember, "The fruit of the Spirit is love." Period.

Allow Christ's love to reign in your heart. After all, what you do is always determined by who you are in Christ, manifested by living the wonderful, Spirit-filled life.

29 ABIDE IN ME

ne of the secrets to living the victorious Spirit-filled life comes in understanding that the fruit of the Spirit is a by-product of His presence in us. Fruit that is picked from a branch is the delectable product of that which is created by the inner life of the vine. On that fateful night as Jesus and His followers moved from the upper room on Mount Zion to the garden of Gethsemane, they passed through the Kidron Valley, crossed a little brook, and journeyed up the sloping side of the Mount of Olives. No doubt they passed by vines and fruit trees that still grow on that holy soil.

I imagine them stopping in the moonlight for a moment as Jesus spoke these words of reminder to them and to us: "Abide in Me, and I in you. As the branch cannot bear fruit of itself, unless it abides in the vine, neither can you, unless you abide in Me. I am the vine, you are the branches. He who abides in Me, and I in him, bears much fruit; for without Me you can do nothing" (John

> Until we discover that we are not the vine but only the branches desperately in need of abiding in the vine, we can do nothing.

15:4–5). Months earlier, back in the Galilean mountains, He had made clear that a person is known "by their fruits" (Matthew 7:20). The fruit any of us may bear as believers in Christ is the evidence of His Spirit abiding in us and we in Him like a vine and a branch. Until we discover that we are not the vine but only the branches desperately in need of abiding in the vine, we can do nothing.

A true disciple of Jesus Christ is a Spirit-filled fruit bearer who is becoming more and more attached to Him and growing daily in grace and knowledge. Peter affirmed that when we come to know the Lord Jesus Christ as our personal Savior, we become "partakers of the divine nature" (2 Peter 1:4). Think of it—we share in the very being of God and in His own divine nature. As Jesus put it in John 15:5, "He who abides in Me, and I in him, bears much fruit." Believers abiding in Christ who share in His very being know three important truths about themselves. They know who they are, where they are, and why they are.

Abiding believers know *who they are.* They are not the vine. They are branches. In this word picture, Jesus made it clear that He, as the vine, is the channel though which the life-producing sap flows into the branches to produce the fruit. Who are we? We are the branches—an extension of the vine for the express purpose of serving the vine in bearing fruit that becomes a blessing to others. If we do not stay connected to the vine, we have no possibility of producing fruit. In fact, without the vine, the branch withers and dies. It can do nothing. True disciples know who they are. They are not the vine. They are the branches.

What is the purpose of a branch—to give shade on a hot day? That's a good thing, but it is not the best thing. Good is often the enemy of the best when it comes to discipleship. Is the purpose of the branch for beauty by being meticulously landscaped? No. Our primary purpose as a branch and the only reason we receive life from the vine is not to benefit ourselves but to bear fruit.

There are times when being a branch can be painful. Jesus said, "Every branch in Me that does not bear fruit He takes away; and every branch that bears fruit He prunes, that it may bear more fruit" (John 15:2). A branch that grows to six feet might be pruned back to a couple feet. The gardener (our heavenly Father) prunes us to rid us of the

> The pruning process can be severe, but it is always for our own good and for the purpose of bearing more fruit.

dead wood of self-pride and ego that limits the amount of life-giving sap that can flow from the vine through us. The pruning process can be severe, but it is always for our own good and for the purpose of bearing more fruit.

Knowing who we are is vital to Christian growth. We are the branches, not the vine. Jesus is the vine, and He longs for the life-giving power of His Holy Spirit to flow through us so that we might produce spiritual fruit for His glory.

Abiding believers also know *where they are.* When a branch is grafted into a vine or tree, it becomes one with the vine. Sap begins to flow out of the vine and into the branch. True followers of Jesus know where they are—they are abiding in the vine. Those who desire to produce spiritual fruit know they must abide in Christ.

This truth comes with a condition. Jesus said, "If you abide in Me, and My words abide in you, you will ask what you desire, and it shall be done for you" (John 15:7). True fruit bearers are those who abide in the living Word, the Lord Jesus, and who have the written Word, the Scriptures, abiding in them. The result is that we can "ask what [we] desire, and it shall be done." This is an astounding claim. How is it possible? If we are abiding in Christ and His Word abides in us, then we are living in such close communion with Him that we would not be moved to ask Him for something that would not be according to His will. And we have and hold to the promise that "if we ask anything according to His will, He hears us . . . [and] we know that we have the petitions that we have asked of Him" (1 John 5:14–15).

Knowing who we are (a branch) and where we are (abiding in the vine) leads us to know *why we are.* Why are we a branch abiding in Christ? To provide shade or produce beauty? No. Jesus said, "By this My Father is glorified, that you bear much fruit; so you will be My disciples" (John 15:8).

True Spirit-filled disciples are aware that their primary purpose in life is to bring glory to their heavenly Father. People judge the worth of a gardener by the fruit of the garden. If you are only interested in receiving your own glory and the applause and praise of those around you, it might be time to examine whether you are truly abiding in Christ. Those who are know why they are here—for the express purpose of bringing glory to God by bearing "much fruit."

> If you are only interested in receiving your own glory and the applause and praise of those around you, it might be time to examine whether you are truly abiding in Christ.

Do you know who you are? Do you know where you are? Do you know why you are? Jesus hit the bull's-eye on a hillside on the northern shore of the Sea of Galilee when He said, "You will know them by their fruits" (Matthew 7:16). Go forth. Abide in Christ. Let His Word abide in you. Produce spiritual fruit, and you will fulfill your utmost purpose—you will bring glory to your Father in heaven.

30 LIFE IN THE SPIRIT

When I was converted to faith in Christ as a teenager, I immediately knew something grand and glorious had taken place inside me. Talk about immediate gratification. I experienced it. It was a "wow" moment for sure. I remember asking one of my new Christian friends, "What has happened to me?" He opened his Bible and pointed me to a verse. I memorized it that day and have held it close to my heart as a life verse throughout these passing decades. This is one of the most personal verses in all the Bible. Like bees on a hive, it swarms with personal pronouns. "I have been crucified with Christ; it is no longer I who live, but Christ lives in me; and the life which I now live in the flesh I live by faith in the Son of God, who loved me and gave Himself for me" (Galatians 2:20).

A life lived in the Spirit is a life that has died to self. Paul concluded his treatise on the fruit of the Spirit with these words, "Those who are Christ's have crucified the flesh with its passions and desires" (Galatians 5:24). No

> Our part now is to reckon ourselves dead indeed to sin and self so that we might live alive unto God through Christ Jesus our Lord.

one has ever produced spiritual fruit without putting self aside and reckoning it as dead. When we entered into Christ, we entered into His death. Our part now is to reckon ourselves dead indeed to sin and self so that we might live alive unto God through Christ Jesus our Lord.

What did Christ do for us when we came to know Him? *He took something from us.* The Bible says, "I have been crucified with Christ." The tense here is perfect, meaning the action was completed in the past with continuing results. The mood is passive, meaning the subject doesn't act; it is the recipient of the action. The apostle goes beyond the acknowledgment that Christ was crucified for me. We have all heard that truth. No, he says, we were crucified *with* Christ. Think of it! After all, we cannot crucify ourselves. We might get our feet nailed and one hand, but not the other. This crucifixion has already been done in the past with continuing action for us in the now. He took our old life from us. We were there—crucified with Christ.

As the Lord Jesus hung there, the crowd saw only one man on that center cross. But God the Father looked down and saw not only Jesus but you and me and everyone who has placed their trust in Christ hanging there with Him. When we come to Christ, God takes our old life from us. We have been "crucified with Christ."

But that is not all. He didn't just take something from me, *He put something in me—my new life!* "It is no longer I who live, but Christ lives in me." This new life we find in Christ is not a reformed life. It is not an improved life. It is not a changed life. It is an *exchanged* life. We give God our old life, and He gives us one that is brand new. Stop for a moment and meditate on this amazing truth—"Christ lives in me!" There is no way to defeat those who truly believe that Christ is alive and, what is more, has taken up permanent residency in our lives. He took something from me (my old life), and He put something in me (my new life)—but there's still more.

He gave something for me—His own life. He loved me and gave Himself for me. These are two realities I wish the whole world could know. God loves us, and He gave Himself for us.

Think of it: *He loved me!* If we could sit down and ask Paul how we can know that Christ loved us, without batting an eye he would reply,

> This new life we find in Christ is not a reformed life. It is not an improved life. It is not a changed life. It is an *exchanged* life.

"He gave Himself for you." Jesus proved His love. He died in my place. His love took my sin so that I could take His own righteousness. He died my death so that I could live His life. He gave Himself for me. He gave Himself for you.

The secret of a Spirit-filled life that produces spiritual fruit is found in our dying to self. But the reality is, that has already been done for us. We cannot crucify ourselves, as hard as we might try. That is why, when writing to the Romans, Paul said, "Reckon yourselves to be dead indeed to sin, but alive to God in Christ Jesus our Lord" (Romans 6:11). Reckon it. Consider it. Count on it.

As I type these words, I am so grateful that my teenage friend did not give me some superficial, feel-good answer to my question. Instead, he pointed me to what became my life verse. It is as real to me today as it was that day I first heard it, so many decades ago now. "I have been crucified with Christ; it is no longer I who live, but Christ lives in me; and the life which I now live in the flesh I live by faith in the Son of God, who loved me and gave Himself for me" (Galatians 2:20). Christ took something from me and gave me something far greater so I could live abiding in Him, filled with His Spirit, and producing much fruit, so that all glory might go to Him who alone is worthy.

31 OUR PRAYER PARTNER: PART ONE

*H*ave you ever wanted a trusted prayer partner, one who not only prays with you but shares your prayer needs, agrees with you in prayer, and believes with you for the answer to your deepest prayer needs? There is good news for you. You do, in fact, have such a prayer partner and may not even be aware of it. He is with you all the time; He searches and knows the innermost recesses of your heart, helps you in your weakness, intercedes for you, and always does so according to God's perfect will. His sweet name is the Holy Spirit, and He lives in you.

The Bible makes this truth crystal clear:

The Spirit also helps in our weaknesses. For we do not know what we should pray for as we ought, but the Spirit Himself makes intercession for us with groanings which cannot be uttered. Now He who searches the hearts knows what the mind of the Spirit is, because He makes intercession for the saints according to the will of God. (Romans 8:26–27)

Let that sink in. *What does the Holy Spirit actually do in us?* He helps us pray (Romans 8:26). This word translated *helps* or *helping* is a very practical word in Greek and means to lend a hand. We find it in the Greek text only one other time in all of Scripture. The scene is in Bethany at the home of Lazarus and his two sisters, Mary and Martha. While Jesus is visiting their home, Martha makes a request of Him. She asks him to tell Mary to help her in the kitchen (Luke 10:40).

This is what the Holy Spirit does for us—He helps us. He lends a hand. He comes alongside us and takes part in our prayers with us, making our prayer life more effective and efficient. The reality is that we are weak and need help, especially when it comes to prayer. We can't find this kind of help in how-to books or prayer journals. We need a prayer partner, and we have one in the Holy Spirit. Just as one might pick up a dish towel and help in the kitchen, the Spirit helps us in our prayer life.

> Just as one might pick up a dish towel and help in the kitchen, the Spirit helps us in our prayer life.

Now, let's consider another question. *Where does He help us?* He helps us "in our weakness." This word is sometimes translated as *crippled* or *invalid* in Scripture. Let's face it. Many of us are not very healthy when it comes to our prayer life. Jesus knows this. After all, His own disciples could not even watch and pray with Him for one hour in His time of greatest need. So He has sent us a prayer partner, the Holy Spirit, to help us where we are weak.

Unfortunately some of us are too proud to admit our weaknesses, much less ask for help. Some "resist the Holy Spirit" (Acts 7:51). Others "grieve the Holy Spirit" (Ephesians 4:30) by never acknowledging their need for help. Still others "quench the Spirit" (1 Thessalonians 5:19) as they continue to seek to live in their own strength.

What does the Holy Spirit do for us? He helps us. Where does He help us? In our weaknesses. This bodes another question: *Why does the Holy Spirit help us in our weakness?* The answer is plain in the text: Because "we do not know what we should pray for as we ought" (Romans 8:26). The Greek word translated as *ought* here appears over one hundred times in the New Testament, but in most of those occurrences, it is translated as *must*. We find this same word in John 3:7 when Jesus admonished, "You must be born again." God brings His plans into being through the prayers of His people. Therefore, it is not so much that we *ought* to pray as it is that we *must* pray.

We should not be surprised that Scripture says we do not know what we should pray for. Even Paul prayed three times for his "thorn in the flesh" to be removed (2 Corinthians 12:7–8) before he realized that God's grace would be sufficient no matter the outcome. We need help. We are weak. Like children, we are not immune from sometimes confusing our wants with our needs, not knowing what is really best for us. We have a prayer partner who helps us in our weaknesses because we simply do not always know how and for what we ought to be praying.

> Like children, we are not immune from sometimes confusing our wants with our needs, not knowing what is really best for us.

Finally, there is a how question: *How does the Holy Spirit help us pray?* Romans 8:26 says He "makes intercession for us." That is, He pleads on our behalf before the Father's throne in heaven. This is how the Holy Spirit moves in our prayer lives. We are weak and must admit it. We do not know how to pray as we ought to pray. So He comes alongside us to help us, to pray with us, for us, and through us, and pleads on our behalf before the Father in heaven.

The key to understanding how the Spirit helps us is that He is the One who knows the mind of God and always prays according to the will of God. He leads us to God's will in our lives. There are many things we know are God's will because they are stated plainly for us in the Bible. But in other matters, we may not have certainty. At this point the Holy Spirit, our prayer partner, comes alongside us and "makes intercession for the saints according to the will of God" (Romans 8:27).

What a comfort to know we are not alone when we pray. We have a prayer partner who helps us. We find God's will through God's Word, trusting in His promises as we yield to the Holy Spirit because He intercedes for us always according to the will of God. And we have a Bible promise that says, "This is the confidence we have in approaching God: that if we ask anything according to his will, he hears us. And if we know that he hears us—whatever we ask—we know that we have what we asked of him" (1 John 5:14–15 NIV).

32 OUR PRAYER PARTNER: PART TWO

*W*hen I first laid eyes on my wife, Susie, it was love at first sight. I remember our first date as if it were last night. Seeking to impress her, I took her to one of the nicest steak restaurants I could find. The last thing I wanted was for her to think I was a bore or someone with whom she might be one-and-done with as a date. So I talked incessantly. Not a minute passed when we were not engaged in conversation, both of us talking without taking a moment to draw a breath. A few months later when I would take her home from a date, we would sit in my car in her parents' driveway for long periods and not a word would be spoken. But we were communicating at a much deeper level than on that first date!

And so it is with our prayer partner, the Holy Spirit. There is a prayer that goes beyond mere words when in fellowship with Him we simply sit quietly and listen to His still, small, loving voice as He speaks to our hearts.

Paul said, "The Spirit also helps in our weaknesses. For we do not know what we should pray for as we ought, but the Spirit Himself makes intercession for us with groanings which cannot be uttered. Now He who searches the hearts knows what the mind of the Spirit is, because He makes intercession for the saints according to the will of God" (Romans 8:26–27). Those of us who know the sweet fellowship that comes with the Holy Spirit know about these "groanings which cannot be uttered." No words . . . just what might be called the prayer of communion.

> Those of us who know the sweet fellowship that comes with the Holy Spirit know about these "groanings which cannot be uttered."

This *prayer of communion* where the Holy Spirit makes intercession for us comes when we have journeyed through the layers of prayer that lead to this moment. My automobile has a navigation system that leads me to my desired destination. I simply insert the address, and it guides me there, telling me when and where to turn, how far I have to go, and even providing an estimated time of arrival.

When the disciples asked the Lord to teach them to pray in Luke 11:1, they were asking for a route, a path that would lead them into the throne room of God's presence in prayer. The Bible clearly lays out this route for us, and it begins with the prayer of confession.

Our sins have separated us from God "so that He will not hear" (Isaiah 59:1–2). David acknowledged that "if I regard iniquity in my heart, the Lord will not hear" (Psalm 66:18). Thus, the obvious place to begin in our prayers is to come clean with Him even as we stand on His promise that "if we confess our sins, He is faithful and just to forgive us our sins and to cleanse us from all unrighteousness" (1 John 1:9). The Bible warns that "he who covers his sins will not prosper." However, the same verse promises that "whoever confesses and forsakes them will have mercy" (Proverbs 28:13). So our prayer path must begin with the *prayer of confession*.

Once we have confessed our sins, we can move on to the *prayer of thanksgiving*. The Bible instructs us to "enter into His gates with thanksgiving, and into His courts with praise" (Psalm 100:4). We cannot fully enter the throne room of prayer unless we pass through the "gates with thanksgiving." Here we pause to thank God for material blessings, particular people,

> Thanksgiving has a liberating effect and is the gate into the Lord's presence in prayer.

172

and spiritual blessings like love, joy, peace, and our own salvation. Thanksgiving has a liberating effect and is the gate into the Lord's presence in prayer.

Once we have entered through the gates of thanksgiving, we can stand in His courts with praise. Here, in expressing our love for Him, we praise Him for His attributes: His goodness, patience, mercy, holiness, and love. We thank God for what He does, and we praise Him for who He is.

Next, this pathway of prayer leads us to the *prayer of intercession*. Here we approach the Lord on behalf of someone else—our family members, friends, pastors, missionaries, political leaders, and so on. Ironically, one of the joys of my life has become offering intercessory prayer for those who have spoken against me or come against me in some form or fashion. In this prayer we especially pray for those who do not know the Lord, pulling down strongholds in their lives of pride or presumption or procrastination, asking the Lord to move in mighty, convicting power upon them.

This leads us to the next level of prayer, the *prayer of petition*. Here we make our petitions, asking Him for anything and everything He may have placed on our hearts. We are to "delight [ourselves] in the LORD" as we trust

Him to give us "the desires of [our] heart" (Psalm 37:4). This does not mean that whatever our heart desires, He will give us. What it does mean is that He gives and grants those desires which have originated with Him and not with us.

After this stop on the pathway of prayer, we arrive at the *prayer of communion*. Here we are simply quiet and still before Him, our Bibles open before us as we listen for His still, small voice speaking for us "with groanings which cannot be uttered." These groanings within us are not verbal. This is not some kind of prayer language. These groanings are silent; they "cannot be uttered." This prayer of communion is the prayer that goes way beyond mere words when we sit still before Him and listen as He speaks to our hearts.

We have a prayer partner, One who knows the will of God, who always knows what is best for us and who "makes intercession for us with groanings which cannot be uttered. . . . He who searches the hearts knows what the mind of the Spirit is, because He makes intercession for the saints according to the will of God" (Romans 8:26–27). Make a friend of the Holy Spirit, and when you pray, invite His presence to pray with you and for you in this prayer of communion that goes beyond mere words.

33 THE HOLY SPIRIT AND POWER: PART ONE

*J*esus had been crucified and buried, had arisen from the grave, had made several appearances to his followers and, finally, had gathered them on the summit of the Mount of Olives east of Jerusalem for a final, physical goodbye. The Bible records the event: "Now when He had spoken these things, while they watched, He was taken up, and a cloud received Him out of their sight. And while they looked steadfastly toward heaven . . . He went up" (Acts 1:9–10). That little band to whom He had given a commission to take the gospel to the ends of the earth watched as He began to levitate and then ascended into the clouds and all the way into heaven itself.

What intrigues me about this event are the words "when He had spoken these things." What things? What did He leave them with? It must have been something vitally important that after all the miracles and manifestations they had seen and heard, He would save these words for the very last. The final words of dying men and women have always been of interest to me. But what did Jesus say here? We are not left to wonder or to speculate. It is recorded for all posterity in the preceding verse. "You shall receive power when the Holy Spirit has come upon you; and you shall be witnesses to Me in Jerusalem, and in all Judea and Samaria, and to the end of the earth" (Acts 1:8).

> Jesus left His followers—and us— with the promise of power. And that power comes when the Holy Spirit comes upon us.

Jesus left them—and us—with the promise of power. And that power comes when the Holy Spirit comes upon us. But power for what? Power in prayer? Power for the working of miracles? Power for the exercising of certain gifts? Power for producing the fruit of the Spirit through our lives? Jesus said the power that He imparts in us through the Holy Spirit is for the express purpose of being witnesses of His saving grace to the "end of the earth."

To begin let's note the *who* of this witnessing power of evangelism. It is given to you. "All of you" is the more proper translation. Those early believers were still looking for a military Messiah, a strong leader who would free them from the iron fist of Rome. In fact, they had just asked, "Lord, will You at this time restore the kingdom to Israel?" (Acts 1:6). After all they had seen they still lived in hopes that He would restore Israel to freedom and political power.

But God had something much more far reaching in mind. His kingdom was going to spread to the "end of the earth." And He would use men and women, Christ's followers down through the generations, starting with that motley group on the mount, to be witnesses of His saving grace. None of us are excused or omitted. "You"—that means them and me and you—"shall receive power when the Holy Spirit has come upon you; and you shall be witnesses to Me" (Acts 1:8).

Jesus not only laid out the *who* of evangelism here but the *what* as well. The promise is that we shall receive power. Isn't this one of our greatest needs in living the Christian life? So many of us are anemic and afraid when it comes to speaking about the very thing we claim most important in life: a personal, saving relationship with Jesus Christ. Yes, we need power!

A few weeks earlier, on the night before the crucifixion, the disciples heard Jesus say, "Most assuredly, I say to you, he who believes in Me, the works that I do he will do also; and greater works than these he will do, because I go to

My Father" (John 14:12–13). And then, on the very heels of that promise came the next one—that when He went back to the Father, He would send "another Helper . . . the Spirit of truth" (John 14:16–17).

That little handful of men and women on the Mount of Olives that day were no different from us. Later they would go out from the upper room on Mount Zion to tell the story of a publicly executed Jew despite all the bigotry and resistance of the Roman rule. How? They had the same supernatural power that is available to us today.

This bring us to another question: *When* would they receive that power? "When the Holy Spirit has come upon you" (Acts 1:8). These early believers had all forsaken Him and fled in the darkness the night of His arrest. Peter denied Him three times in the courtyard of the high priest. Their record of unreserved faithfulness was no better than many of ours. So what happened between then and this point? What caused their sudden and dramatic transformation from cowardice to courage? What enabled Peter, as well as the rest of the apostles, to suddenly live with such boldness that, remembering the question of Jesus—"Will you lay down your life for My sake?" (John 13:38)—they willingly met their own martyrs' deaths? God the Father had sent the same Spirit that raised Christ from the dead to take up residence in each of them with supernatural power (Romans 8:11). And this same Spirit lives today in each and every believer.

Who? You, me, all of us. Every believer. *What?* We will receive power. *When?* When the Holy Spirit comes upon us. If you are saved, the Holy Spirit is upon you. He lives in you. Therefore, you have the power you need to live the victorious Christian life. There is no such thing as a true believer in Christ who does not have power.

> What enabled the apostles to suddenly live with such boldness that they willingly met their own martyrs' deaths? I'll tell you what happened— the Holy Spirit had come upon them, and with Him came that promised power!

34 THE HOLY SPIRIT AND POWER: PART TWO

*J*esus' last words on this earth were these: "You shall receive power when the Holy Spirit has come upon you; and you shall be witnesses to Me in Jerusalem, and in all Judea and Samaria, and to the end of the earth" (Acts 1:8). This brings us to a *why* question. Why do we receive power when the Holy Spirit comes upon us? Is there an express purpose? Jesus did not say we would receive power through the Holy Spirit so we could manifest miraculous, nature-defying miracles. He didn't say we would walk on water like He did or multiply small lunches to feed multitudes of hungry people or even raise the dead like He once did in Bethany. Jesus said the Holy Spirit's power is provided to us for the express purpose of being "witnesses to Me in Jerusalem, and in all Judea and Samaria, and to the end of the earth."

If you are a true believer, you have Christ. If you have Christ, you have the Holy Spirit. If you have the Holy Spirit, you have power. If you have power, you will be a witness of His saving grace to a lost and dying world.

> If you have the Holy Spirit, you have power. If you have power, you will be a witness of His saving grace to a lost and dying world.

The analogy of a court of law is apropos here. Jesus said we are to be His witnesses. In a trial a witness is someone who takes a seat on the witness stand, pledges to tell the truth before the judge and jury, and simply speaks about what they personally know or saw or heard about the matter at hand. You did not receive power to be the judge, sitting in judgment of someone else. You did not receive power to be the prosecuting attorney, pointing a finger of accusation at others. Nor did you receive power to be the defense attorney, seeking to build a case that leads to reasonable doubt. You are not the jury, sitting there trying to decide what is right or wrong. "You shall be *witnesses* to Me" (emphasis added). We are filled with God's Spirit and power to tell what we know of the Lord Jesus Christ by personal experience, to press the claims of Christ upon the hearts of anyone who will hear, and then, to leave the results to God.

We derive the English word *martyr* from the same Greek word translated *witness* in Acts 1:8. A martyr lays down his or her life for their faith. The men and women who first heard these words on the Mount of Olives that day descended the mountain to indeed become martyrs in the truest sense. Simon Peter was crucified upside down. James was killed at the sword of King Herod. Thomas took these words to heart, went to India to be a witness, and was killed at the point of a spear. By the thousands these early followers of Christ witnessed about His saving grace with their dying words.

Jesus is still calling us to be "witnesses to Me." We are not some slick group of recruiters trying to get people to join our club. We are not salesmen trying to persuade people to buy our product. We are to be witnesses to everyone everywhere of Christ's saving grace, and we have been given His power to accomplish the task. It is a marvel that God entrusted His glorious gospel to a group of common, hardworking fishermen and their friends. And it is a marvel that He is still entrusting it to people like you and me. But He did, and He does. And He gives us the supernatural power to be His witnesses when the Holy Spirit comes to dwell within us.

> Jesus is still calling us to be "witnesses to Me."

This brings us finally to a *where* question. Where are

we to be His witnesses? To everyone, everywhere. In our own city, our own country, and across all the continents, even to the end of the earth. Jesus' plan is for total participation (all of us) and total penetration (to the end of the earth) until there is no one left who has not heard witness of the gospel of Christ.

The early believers were to begin in Jerusalem. All the talk of Jesus being alive would not sit well with the Sanhedrin, the council of Jewish leaders responsible for His execution. It likely would have been easier to start over in Asia Minor. But Jesus was fully cognizant of the fact that if we can't be witnesses of the gospel at home, we can't be witnesses anywhere. So, they started at home. And this ragtag group fulfilled Acts 1:8 in their lifetime. How? By the supernatural power of the Holy Spirit emboldening them to be witnesses, to speak of what they had seen and heard.

This challenge from the lips of our Lord calls us to penetrate the entire world with the gospel. No one is excluded. Every religion is to be confronted. Every error is to be exposed. Every language is to be translated. Every tribe is to be visited. As the songwriter H. Ernest Nichol wrote, "We've a story to tell to the nations, that shall turn their hearts to the right," and we are to tell it till "the darkness shall turn to the dawning, and the dawning to noonday light, and Christ's great kingdom shall come to earth, the kingdom of love and light."

If you think that is a big task for us today, think about what it was for those who first heard it. Talk about a mission unaccomplished—on the surface it appeared impossible in every way. It seemed physically impossible: there were hardly any roads, much less any modern means of travel. It seemed legally impossible: it was against the law to teach or preach in the name of Jesus, and many early believers were incarcerated and brought to a martyr's death because of it. It seemed socially impossible too: many of these people were discards and rejects. But God revealed that "not many wise . . . not many mighty, not many noble, are called. But God has chosen the foolish things of the world to put to shame the wise . . . that no flesh should glory in His presence. But . . . that, as it is written, 'He who glories, let him glory in the LORD'" (1 Corinthians 1:26–27, 29–31).

That early group of believers turned their world upside down. They did so much with what seemed so little. But they had power derived from the Holy Spirit for the express purpose of filling the entire world with the message of Christ's love and His call to salvation.

If you have the Holy Spirit, *you have power*! Power,

right now, to be His witness. The gospel is alive today and still powerful because generation after generation across these past twenty centuries have received His power and been His witnesses. Someone you know needs a witness of God's saving grace today.

35 THE HOLY SPIRIT AND THE UNPARDONABLE SIN: PART ONE

*S*ome of the most astonishing words ever to fall from the lips of Jesus were these:

> Every sin and blasphemy will be forgiven men, but the blasphemy against the Spirit will not be forgiven men. Anyone who speaks a word against the Son of Man, it will be forgiven him; but whoever speaks against the Holy Spirit, it will not be forgiven him, either in this age or in the age to come. (Matthew 12:31–32)

We present the free offer of the gospel as one of full pardon. But Jesus says that all sins will indeed be forgiven *except one*! There is a sin that when committed is unpardonable and will never, ever be forgiven.

Is it the sin of murder? David, the greatest king in Israel's history, the "man after [God's] own heart" (Acts

13:22), committed this sin. And what about the man who gave us almost half our New Testament from his own pen, the apostle Paul? He oversaw the murder of Stephen outside the Lions' Gate of the walled city of Jerusalem. But neither David nor Paul committed the unpardonable sin. It is not murder.

Is it adultery? Once Jesus came upon a woman about to be stoned who had been taken in the very act of adultery by the religious police. Upon dismissing her accusers, He looked into her face and spoke these warm and welcoming words: "Neither do I condemn you; go and sin no more" (John 8:11). And what about the woman at the well in Sychar of Samaria? He told her all the sordid things she had ever done and then offered her living water and forgiveness (John 4:13–14). Adultery is not the unpardonable sin.

Is it robbery? No. Zacchaeus cheated and robbed people over a lifetime but found grace in the eyes of the Lord (Luke 19:9–10). Is it lying? If it is, Simon Peter was in a heap of trouble. He lied about the fact of ever knowing our Lord (Matthew 26:73–75). What about the sin of unbelief? If so, Thomas is guilty (John 20:25). We've even given him a name that sticks to him like glue: Doubting Thomas.

What then is this sin that Jesus calls unpardonable? Many who have not committed this sin are afraid they have. If you are afraid you may have committed it, you can rest assured that you have not done so, for your very concern is proof positive that the Holy Spirit is still at work in your heart. However, there are many today in deep danger of committing it.

This sin is not against the Father or the Son; it is against the Holy Spirit. It is the one and only sin that once committed has *no* forgiveness—yet so many Christians are entirely ignorant of what it is. Let's begin by examining what it means to commit this unpardonable sin.

The basic meaning of the word *forgive* is "to send away." Upon our confession of faith and repentance, God takes our sins and "sends them away" from us forever. This same word is used when talking about how James and John left their father and the others in the boat to follow Jesus. It is used to describe how the fever that plagued Peter's mother-in-law in Capernaum "left" her when she felt the healing touch of Jesus (Mark 1:29–31). God takes our sins and sends them away; He separates them from us "as far as the east is from the west" (Psalm 103:12) and "will remember [them] no more" (Hebrews 8:12).

Jesus sends all our sins away. But there is one sin that

will never be sent away, never be forgiven, never be pardoned. What is it? Jesus calls it the sin of "blasphemy against the Spirit" (Matthew 12:31). Some say this is the act of ascribing to Satan what is actually a work of the Lord. In other words, declaring that something that is of God is not really of God. If this is true, then Saul of Tarsus, who became the apostle Paul, committed it. He made known to all his belief that what was happening in the early church was not of God and was an affront to the traditions of their religion. In his letter to Timothy, he confessed, "I was once a blasphemer and a persecutor . . . [but] was shown mercy because I acted in ignorance and unbelief" (1 Timothy 1:13 NIV). Paul's sin was pardoned, so attributing a word or action from God as coming from Satan cannot be the unpardonable sin. And who of us in some way or another over the years has not done something to this effect?

> Jesus sends all our sins away. But there is one sin that will never be sent away, never be forgiven, never be pardoned.

The unpardonable sin is not an *act*; it is an *attitude*. It is a conscious and willful rejection of the saving power and grace of God toward all men. To blaspheme the Holy Spirit is to have an attitude that rejects the Holy Spirit's witness in your heart. And when a person reaches this point, his sin becomes unpardonable, and he is without hope.

Why is this sin against the Holy Spirit unpardonable? It is not because the Holy Spirit is *greater* than the Father or the Son. I believe it is because He is *later* in the sense of this aspect of His ministry among us. The Holy Spirit is God's final attempt to reach your soul with salvation. The Father revealed His redemptive plan throughout history. The Son, the Lord Jesus, came to carry it out by His substitutionary death on the cross. Finally, the Holy Spirit comes to convict us of sin, convince us of righteousness, lift up Christ, point us to Him, and call and lead us to salvation. No one is coming after the Holy Spirit. He is God Himself going as far as He will go to save you without forcing His will on you and making you a puppet rather than a person.

The unpardonable sin, then, is the constant, consistent, willful rejection of the Holy Spirit's witness to your heart. There comes a time in a man or woman's heart when they have said no to Christ so many times "because of the blindness of their heart," that they become "past feeling" (Ephesians 4:18–19). We derive our word *callus* from this Greek phrase, "past feeling." It is actually a medical term for skin that has lost its sensitivity and ceases to feel pain.

Most of us have had a callus on our foot or hand into

which we could stick a pin and feel no pain. This is what happens to someone's heart when over and over they reject God's call. Each time they reject Him, the "callus" on their heart becomes a bit harder, and after a while it is not that the Holy Spirit ceases to knock but that they can

> The unpardonable sin is the constant, consistent, willful rejection of the Holy Spirit's witness to your heart.

no longer hear. They have become past feeling. Those are haunting words, *past feeling*.

The unpardonable sin is an attitude, not some single, isolated act. It is committed against the Holy Spirit, not because He is greater but because He is later. He is God's last attempt to bring you to salvation. And those who continue to willfully reject or neglect His call to their hearts of the testimony of Jesus eventually commit this one sin that is unpardonable. No wonder the Bible exhorts, "Now is the accepted time; behold, now is the day of salvation" (2 Corinthians 6:2). There will not always be adequate time. God forgives all our sin in Jesus' name, except for one!

36 THE HOLY SPIRIT AND THE UNPARDONABLE SIN: PART TWO

*H*aving observed in the preceding chapter *what* the unpardonable sin is and *how* it is committed, we now turn our attention to *who* actually commits it. Jesus said, "Every sin and blasphemy will be forgiven men, but the blasphemy against the Spirit will not be forgiven men. Anyone who speaks a word against the Son of Man, it will be forgiven him; but whoever speaks against the Holy Spirit, it will not be forgiven him, either in this age or in the age to come" (Matthew 12:31–32).

This is serious business, to think that God, who promises to forgive and cleanse us of all sin (1 John 1:9), warns that there is one—and only one—sin that will find no forgiveness from Him. This sin is not committed as a single act but is an attitude of the heart: it is the perpetual and willful rejection of the Holy Spirit's witness of Jesus to our hearts.

But who actually commits this sin? Can someone who has genuinely been converted by receiving God's grace and placing their trust in Christ alone through repentance and faith ever commit the unpardonable sin? Some believers are afraid they may have actually committed it. Let me state this here as clearly as I can—*No true believer in Christ has ever committed the unpardonable sin.* Period. Full stop. Further, no unbeliever who is being convicted of their sin has committed it. No truly sincere seeker after God has committed it. These are all indications that the Holy Spirit is still working in your life. Had you actually committed this sin, you would not care. You would be, in Paul's words, "past feeling" (Ephesians 4:19).

As a reminder, the unpardonable sin is not an act as much as it is an attitude. We are living in a dispensation of grace, one in which the Holy Spirit is here, active in our lives, and never abandoning us. The only person who ends up finally being abandoned by God is the one who has totally abandoned God himself, the one who has said no to the call of Christ so many, many times that the still, small voice of the Holy Spirit can no longer be heard.

> The unpardonable sin is not an act as much as it is an attitude.

The unpardonable sin can be avoided. There are several

danger signs which should be noted. There is the danger of *procrastination*. Some simply postpone responding to God's call until gradually, subtly, any sense of urgency subsides. There is the danger of *assumption*. Some simply assume they will be able to choose the time and place when they will get right with God. But they are ignoring the conviction of the Holy Spirit, and there may come a time when they no longer sense a need. For still others, there is the danger of *presumption*. These people are holding on to some "decision" they made long ago; they are pretending in their mind that all is well. They may even join the church and die with a perfect-attendance button pinned to their lapel. One of the devil's most subtle schemes is deceiving us into presuming that all is well.

Those who have committed the unpardonable sin will not be plagued by a lack of peace of mind. Quite the contrary; they are past all that; they are "past feeling." Their hearts have become so hardened through continuous neglect that they have moved beyond the reach of spiritual truth.

Years ago, I heard the story of a young man in another day and another time who left the farm to work in the big city. He promised his mother he would find a church and attend while away. He gave her his solemn word, left home, and moved to the city. After being there awhile, he took a horseback ride on a Sunday. He had remembered his promise but had never carried it out. Riding through a little village, he passed a church with its bells ringing in the bell tower, calling people to worship. The bells convicted him of his promise, but he kept riding. He stopped when he could still only barely hear the sound. They spoke to his heart as he noticed the farther he rode, the fainter their sound. If he rode any farther, he would ride beyond the sound of the bells. He made the decision to go back to the little church while he could still hear the bells calling him to worship.

Many of us, in times past, have heard the call of the Holy Spirit in our hearts to come to Jesus. He is still calling. Perhaps some can only barely still sense Him. If so, it is not too late.

Why did Jesus call this sin—out of all the evil humankind can perpetrate—the one that is unpardonable? Clearly because no one can be saved without the operation and activity of the Holy Spirit. It is not that He is greater than the Father or the Son. It is because He is later. He is God's last attempt to bring you to salvation. The Bible says, "Therefore I make known to you that no one speaking by the Spirit of God calls Jesus accursed, and no one can say that Jesus is Lord except by the Holy Spirit" (1 Corinthians 12:3). To reject the Holy Spirit's final witness of Christ to your heart is to reject Jesus Himself. And that is life's greatest and only unpardonable sin.

37 WITH YOU ALWAYS

*P*romises made are valuable. But promises kept are invaluable. We do not have to journey very far along the path of life before we discover this truth. We have all had promises made to us that were never carried out, never kept. Or perhaps we've made those promises ourselves. A promise is not worth much until it is fulfilled. Jesus left us with a multitude of promises, but there was never one more needed and held closer to the heart than the one He made in the upper room to His confused and conflicted followers. He had just told them that He was about to leave them, but then He gave them this promise: "I will pray the Father, and He will give you another Helper, that *He may abide with you forever*—the Spirit of truth" (John 14:16–17, emphasis added). *Forever* means what it says—forever and always.

A few days later, just before He ascended back to heaven from the Mount of Olives, "He commanded them . . . to wait for the Promise of the Father, 'which,' He said, 'you have heard from Me'" (Acts 1:4). And so, they carried His promise back to the upper room where they waited until it became a promise kept. They would never again see Christ the way they had seen Him that day on the Mount of Olives. That is, in the same visible, material, touchable body. No longer would He walk on the road from Jerusalem to Jericho with them. No longer would their children feel His tender hands of blessing upon their heads. No longer would they be able to look into those piercing and penetrating eyes. No longer would they hear His authoritative yet tender voice.

After the ascension, the disciples went back to the upper room to await the arrival of God's promise. I'm sure they missed Him as they waited there, but they still remembered some of the last words He spoke to them: "It is to your advantage that I go away; for if I do not go away, the Helper [Holy Spirit] will not come to you; but if I depart, I will send Him to you" (John 16:7).

They did not retreat to that hidden place to wait until they were worthy to receive the Spirit. Who of us is worthy? They went back simply to wait, and as they waited, they prayed, and as they prayed, they came into "one accord" (Acts 1:14)—they got right with each other. Think about who was among them. Peter was there, fresh from his denial just a few days earlier. Thomas was there. He had doubted Jesus on more than one occasion. James and John were there. They had argued over who was the greatest among them and even sent their mother to advocate for them to Jesus Himself. Mary Magdalene was there. Some of them thought less of her because she was from a town known for prostitution. I believe Nicodemus might have been with them too. He'd retrieved the body of Christ from the cross for a proper burial, but could he really be trusted?

What a strange mix of people—wealthy, illiterate, those with tarnished and questionable pasts. But differences got settled as they waited. Hurts were shared. Apologies were accepted. Reconciliation took place. They all came into "one accord," and when that happens, the Holy Spirit has His own way of showing up. And show up He did, filling them with power and the promise to "abide with them forever."

The Holy Spirit is with you right now, even as you hold this book in your hands. Long ago King David asked the Lord, "Where can I go from Your Spirit? Or where can I flee from Your presence? If I ascend into heaven, You are there; if I make my bed in hell, behold, You

> The Holy Spirit is with you right now, even as you hold this book in your hands.

are there. If I take the wings of the morning, and dwell in the uttermost parts of the sea, even there Your hand shall lead me" (Psalm 139:7–10). There is no place we can go, no place we can hide, where He is not present.

This is the point of Jesus' last words immediately before He left for heaven. "Lo, I am with you always," He said, "even to the end of the age" (Matthew 28:20). Paul referred to the Holy Spirit as "the Spirit of God" and "the Spirit of Christ" in Romans 8:9. He also called Him the "Spirit of Jesus Christ" in Philippians 1:19. The Holy Spirit is the person of God who abides within us and never leaves. If Jesus were still here in the flesh, He would lead us, love us, guide us, teach us, encourage us at every turn. But now, more than just being *with* us, He *lives in* us every moment of every day in the person of His Spirit, the Holy Spirit.

There is nowhere you can go that He is not there. If you have not yet come to know Jesus as your personal Savior, the Holy Spirit is there, pointing you to Jesus, convicting you of your sin, convincing you of Christ's righteousness, and knocking on your heart's door. If you have received Christ, then He is alive this moment in you—and what is more, He is with you now and forever. He will never leave you nor forsake you. He made a promise to you—and like all His promises, He kept it!

38 WHO IS ON YOUR SIDE?

*A*mong my fondest childhood memories are the weekly Saturday morning football games on the old vacant lot in my neighborhood. We would pick two captains, and then they would choose their teams, one pick after another. There was one kid in particular that everyone wanted on their team. He was bigger and faster than the rest of us, not to mention much tougher as well. When he was on your side, you knew you were going to win.

Some of us are totally unaware that in the game of life, we have Someone very powerful on our side. That Someone happens to be the Holy Spirit. Before Jesus left the earth to ascend to His Father, He spoke these words: "I will pray the Father, and He will give you another Helper, that He may abide with you forever—the Spirit of truth, whom the world cannot receive, because it neither sees Him nor knows Him; but you know Him, for He dwells with you and will be in you" (John 14:16–17).

We have the Holy Spirit on our side. Jesus refers to Him as the Helper. The Greek noun *Paraclete* literally means "the one who comes beside us." Have you ever been accused of something you did not do? Or maybe you did do it, and you had to admit it. Maybe you were taken to court, and you were standing before the judge, alone and afraid. And then someone came to stand beside you and, speaking on your behalf, proved your innocence before the judge.

That attorney standing by your side perfectly illustrates the word picture the Lord uses in this Scripture.

We have the Holy Spirit on our side. Jesus refers to Him as the Helper.

In essence He was saying, "I'm leaving you, but I will send you another Helper, a Counselor or Advocate, to stand beside you and to be on your side." Jesus continues to affirm that this Advocate is, indeed, the Holy Spirit who came first to convict and convert, and now to counsel, comfort, console, and eventually complete us.

The key to understanding all of this is in the adjective "another." You will be given *another* Helper. In the language of the New Testament, there are two distinct Greek words translated as "another." One means another of a *different* kind, while the other means another of the *same* kind, the same make and model. If I held up a Montblanc writing pen in one hand and, in the other hand, a plastic Bic pen, I would use the first word. That is, here is a pen and here is another pen, but they are different in every way. One is expensive and the other is cheap. One is polished and attractive while the other is simple and plastic. Still, they are both pens. Conversely, if I held up that same Montblanc writing pen but in the other hand held up one that was identical to it, I would still say, "Here is a pen, and here is one just like it." If I were speaking in Greek, I would use the second word referenced above.

What is the point? Which word do you suppose Jesus used when mentioning He was leaving but "another" would come in His place who would never leave? He used the latter word. Essentially, Jesus was saying, "The Holy Spirit is coming, but He is the same make and model as Me. We are identical."

This truth is all wrapped up in the mystery we call the Trinity. Being monotheistic, we believe in only one God. We don't worship three distinct gods. The Lord is one, manifested in three persons: the Father, the Son, and the Holy Spirit. The Father is the *source* of all things. The Son is the *course*—through Him the work of creation and salvation is accomplished. And the Spirit is the *force* behind it all. He inspired the Bible writers. He convicts us of our sin. He is the agent in conversion. He indwells us, gifts us, and fills us for the Christian life. If you want to know what God is like, look at Jesus. If you want to know what the Holy Spirit is like, look at Jesus. And, good news! He is on your side. When Jesus told His followers that the Father would send *another* Helper, He was telling them that the Holy Spirit and He were the same—the same make, the same model, the same God.

The precious Spirit of truth, the Holy Spirit, is not just *by* your side; He is *on* your side. Not only in your time of crisis or simply for a moment from time to time—He abides with you *forever* and, as Jesus promised "He dwells with you and will be in you" (John 14:17). The apostle John pinpointed it further in his epistle: "If anyone sins, we have an Advocate with the Father, Jesus Christ the righteous" (1 John 2:1). The Holy Spirit chose you to be on His forever team. He is faithful to His promise not just to be by your side, but on your side.

39 IT'S NOT WHERE YOU ARE BUT WHOSE YOU ARE

*L*ife often finds us in a difficult spot. It certainly did for John. Now over ninety years of age, and the only apostle who did not meet a violent and vicious martyr's death, we find him exiled on an island called Patmos off the coast of Asia Minor and in the middle of the Aegean Sea. But this was not some tropical retirement vacation home on a beautiful island like Capri or Mykonos. Patmos was a barren, volcanic rock of an island. As the aged apostle began to write the book of Revelation, he said, "I . . . was on the island that is called Patmos . . . [but] I was in the Spirit on the Lord's Day" (Revelation 1:9–10). What is the message he is seeking to convey? It's not *where* you are that matters most; it is *Whose* you are.

Patmos is a lonely, mostly uninhabited rock of an island off the coast of Asia Minor. Think Alcatraz. Ten miles long and six miles wide, it is rough, desolate, and depressing. The Romans used it as a dumping ground for all sorts of criminals. When their mighty legions conquered a country with their iron fist of submission, they emptied all the prisons as well as the mental institutions, placed those people on boats, sailed them to Patmos, and dumped them there to die. It was like a zoo filled with wild human beings.

Caesar had placed images of himself in all the conquered lands, demanding that the people bow down and express their allegiance to Rome, confessing that "Caesar is lord." Those who refused met terrible fates. Polycarp, the famed preacher in Smyrna, refused and was burned at the stake. Ignatius, the pastor of the great missionary church in Antioch, met his death at the jaws of wild animals. They and thousands of other early believers insisted there was no Lord but Jesus and met similar fates.

John, once the carefree Galilean fisherman, the one who leaned on Jesus' breast in the upper room, the one who stood by Mary at the cross, was now over ninety years of age and banished to Patmos to live out his remaining days in the company of criminals and the mentally ill from all over the Mediterranean world. But it was there that the aged apostle penned the final book of our Bible—the book of Revelation. After customary greetings, John turned the attention to himself, saying, "I . . . was on the island that is called Patmos" (Revelation 1:9).

He was "on the island that is called Patmos." There is so much behind that simple statement. Patmos was a place of liabilities, limitations, and loneliness, to name just three. He could have elaborated, asking his readers to commiserate with his deplorable situation, but he didn't. Instead, he continued, saying he was on Patmos "for the word of God and for the testimony of Jesus Christ." Then he added: "I was in the Spirit on the Lord's Day" (Revelation 1:9–10).

You may be in a difficult season of life yourself. Look at John. Listen to him. He leaves us with a word of hope and encouragement. Many of us live in the "I was on the island of Patmos" syndrome and see nothing but the problems. When we can move on to say "I was in the Spirit," we can begin a new adventure by holding to the Bible promise, "Where the Spirit of the Lord is, there is liberty" (2 Corinthians 3:17). As John will show us, it doesn't matter where we are or what our circumstances are. What matters most is whose we are.

> You may be in a difficult season of life yourself. Look at John. Listen to him. He leaves us with a word of hope.

On Patmos we see *liabilities.* The surroundings were adverse. The people around John would have been dangerous and frightening. He had to scrounge for food and to find a safe place to sleep at night. Perhaps on the shores of your personal Patmos, the sun beats down upon you and pounds you with liabilities. It's easy to fall into the "I was on the island of Patmos" syndrome and focus only on the liabilities. But stop. That's only half the story.

When John continued with "I was in the Spirit on the Lord's Day," his focus shifted from his surroundings to the Holy Spirit, and all those limitations gave way to lordship. John saw purpose. Jesus had allowed his experience for a divine reason. Immediately after John's confession, the Holy Spirit spoke in a "loud voice, as of a trumpet, saying . . . 'What you see, write in a book and send it to the . . . churches'" (Revelation 1:10–11). And thus, we have the last book of the Bible, the book of Revelation, the Apocalypse.

Liabilities can be lost in the lordship of Jesus Christ. It is not *where* you are. It is *whose* you are that matters most.

On Patmos we also see *limitations*. John was "on the island that is called Patmos." Talk about limitations—the place was full of them. Every morning John looked out, and all he saw was the sea beyond. At night when he pillowed his head on some rock, his last sight was the moonlight bouncing off the waves of the sea. He was isolated, cut off, with no control. He could not sit with friends, walk in the marketplace, hear news from home, or read his books.

Many live on their own Patmos today, feeling isolated from what they know and love and seeing only the limitations their circumstances have caused.

But wait. Again, that's only half the story! "I was in the Spirit on the Lord's Day." When John's focus changed, all his liabilities gave way to liberty. He was not a prisoner. He was free. The words of Jesus took on deeper meaning: "You shall know the truth, and the truth shall make you free" (John 8:32). If you're on Patmos today, all your liabilities can be turned into liberty too. Most of us never get our focus off verse nine to move on to verse ten, but when we do and we exclaim with John, "I was in the Spirit," we discover that it is not where we are, after all, but whose we are that brings lordship and liberty.

> If you're on Patmos today, all your liabilities can be turned into liberty too.

Finally, on Patmos we also see *loneliness*. When John declared that he was on the island called Patmos, loneliness was threaded through every syllable. His companions were a bunch of hard-hearted, embittered men. How he must have missed the fellowship of his family and friends. So many in our busy world today are experiencing loneliness. It's easy to fall into the "I was on the island of Patmos" syndrome and be consumed with loneliness.

But stop again. That's *still* only half the story. When John moved from verse nine to verse ten, all his loneliness gave way to love. In Romans 8:35, Paul asked, "Who shall separate us from the love of Christ? Shall tribulation, or distress, or persecution, or famine, or nakedness, or peril, or sword?" All those things were on Patmos. But John realized that, with the Holy Spirit, he could not lose, and I think, like Paul, he came to this conclusion: "I am persuaded that neither death nor life, nor angels nor principalities nor powers, nor things present nor things to come, nor height nor depth, nor any other created thing, shall be able to separate [me] from the love of God which is in Christ Jesus [my] Lord" (Romans 8:38–39). Yes, even loneliness can be lost in the love of God.

Perhaps you've been living in verse nine with your eyes only on your personal Patmos. The time has come to make verse ten your own confession—"I was in the Spirit on the Lord's Day." Say it. And when you do, you will find out with John that all those liabilities will be turned into lordship, your limitations into liberty, and your loneliness into love.

After all, it's not where you are. It's *Whose* you are that matters most.

40 THE SPIRIT AND THE BRIDE SAY "COME"

*T*he Holy Spirit beckons us to come to the Lord Jesus Christ. On the last page of the Bible, we read, "The Spirit and the bride say, 'Come!' And let him who hears say, 'Come!' And let him who thirsts come. Whoever desires, let him take the water of life freely" (Revelation 22:17). The bride is a clear reference to the church in the New Testament, that body of born-again believers who one day will be reunited with the Bridegroom, our Lord Jesus Christ. We who are alive in this day are in partnership with the Holy Spirit, offering the lost world the free invitation of the gospel to come to Jesus. While the church issues the outward call, the Holy Spirit issues the inward call to the heart. We work in tandem: The Spirit and the bride say, "Come!"

> While the church issues the outward call, the Holy Spirit issues the inward call to the heart. We work in tandem: The Spirit and the bride say, "Come!"

The Holy Spirit pleads with us to come to Jesus. This is the *inward call* to our hearts. I could beg you on my knees with tears in my eyes as I described the horrors of hell and the wonders of heaven—but you will never come to Jesus unless the Holy Spirit is drawing you. Our Lord Himself said, "No one can come to Me unless the Father who sent Me draws him" (John 6:44). Immediately after Peter made the great confession at Caesarea Philippi, Jesus pronounced a blessing on him, saying, "Flesh and blood has not revealed this to you, but My Father who is in heaven" (Matthew 16:17). Later, the apostle Paul would add, "For as many as are led by the Spirit of God, these are the sons of God" (Romans 8:14). And to the Galatians, Paul said that "it pleased God, who separated me from my mother's womb [to call] me through His grace" (Galatians 1:15).

Not to be left out, Peter weighed in, saying, "You are a chosen generation . . . His own special people, that you may proclaim the praises of Him who called you out of darkness into His marvelous light" (1 Peter 2:9). He ended that same epistle with the reminder that "the God of all grace [had] called us to His eternal glory by Christ Jesus" (1 Peter 5:10). The Holy Spirit is God's agent in calling us to Himself. "The Spirit . . . [says,] Come!"

Earlier in this volume, we saw the partnership we have

with the Holy Spirit as our prayer partner. Here we see our partnership with Him in calling men and women to faith in Christ. Through the Holy Spirit we hear the inward call to our hearts. Through the church, the bride of Christ, we hear the *outward call.*

We see this partnership in the little village of Bethany at the grave of Lazarus. Lazarus had died and was already buried when Jesus arrived on the scene. He was greeted by a funeral party in deep mourning. An outward call was given—something for the people there at the grave to do. Their job was to roll away the large stone that sealed the grave. But it wasn't until Jesus spoke that Lazarus was brought back to life. Thus, our Lord issued the *inward call* as He cried, "Lazarus, come forth!" (John 11:43). And he did.

Our job in the outward call today is to roll away stones. As we issue the outward call for people to come to faith in Christ, we seek to roll away stones of indifference, unbelief, presumption, pride, procrastination, and the like. Our apologetics and our witness enable men and women to be more sensitive to hearing the Spirit's inward call to their hearts. We are in

> We are in partnership with the Holy Spirit in life's greatest task of calling people to faith in Christ.

partnership with the Holy Spirit in life's greatest task of calling people to faith in Christ.

The Spirit says come. In many ways, the words of this book are the outward call. Can you hear the Spirit's inward call to your own heart right now? Listen for what the prophet Elijah called a "still small voice" (1 Kings 19:12 KJV). Oh, it's not an audible voice. But when you hear it, you'll know—it's unmistakable. Jesus is calling for you.

EPILOGUE

*I*t's possible that the Holy Spirit has been speaking directly to you as you read this volume. He's been leading you to put your faith and trust in Christ alone for your eternal salvation. Heaven is God's free gift to you. It cannot be earned. It is not deserved. We all have something in common—we are all sinners, and we cannot save ourselves. We have all fallen short of God's perfect standard for our lives. He is a God of love and does not want to punish us for our sins. Yet He is also a God of justice and cannot clear the guilty.

This is where Jesus steps into the equation. He is the infinite God-Man who came to take our sins in His own body on the cross. Jesus, who knew no sin, *became sin for us* "that we might become the righteousness of God in Him" (2 Corinthians 5:21). It's not enough to know these facts though. We must individually, by faith, transfer our trust from ourselves and our own human effort to Christ alone and put our faith in Him for our personal salvation.

The Lord Jesus said, "Behold, I stand at the door and knock. If anyone hears My voice and opens the door, I will come in to him" (Revelation 3:20). That "voice" is the inward call of the Holy Spirit to you. Jesus promised, "Whoever calls on the name of the LORD shall be saved" (Romans 10:13). If that is the desire of your heart, you can call on Him right now. A prayer cannot save you, but Jesus can when you call upon Him. The following is a suggested prayer:

Dear Lord Jesus,
I know I have sinned and do not deserve eternal life in and of myself. Thank You for dying on the cross for me. Thank You for calling me to Yourself by the Holy Spirit. Please forgive my sins and come into my life. I turn to You and place my total trust in You. I accept Your free gift of eternal life. Thank You for coming into my life. In Jesus' name I pray, amen.

If you said this prayer and it expressed the true desire of your heart, you can now claim the promise that Jesus made to those who believe in Him—"Most assuredly, I say to you, he who believes in Me has everlasting life" (John 6:47).

Welcome to God's forever family. The Holy Spirit has immersed you into the body of Christ, and you are now entering life's greatest adventure—getting to know Christ with the promise that His Holy Spirit now lives in you and will never, ever leave or forsake you.

ABOUT THE AUTHOR

O. S. Hawkins, a native of Fort Worth, Texas, is a graduate of Texas Christian University (BBA) and Southwestern Baptist Theological Seminary (MDiv, PhD). He is chancellor and senior professor of pastoral ministry and evangelism at Southwestern Baptist Theological Seminary. He is the former pastor of the historic First Baptist Church in Dallas, Texas, and is president emeritus of GuideStone Financial Resources, the world's largest Christian-screened mutual fund, serving 250,000 church workers and Christian university personnel with an asset base exceeding twenty billion dollars, where he served as president/CEO from 1997–2022.

Hawkins is the author of more than fifty books, including the bestselling *Joshua Code* and the entire Code Series of devotionals published by HarperCollins/Thomas Nelson, which have sold more than two million copies. He preaches in churches and conferences across the nation. He and his wife, Susie, have two daughters, two sons-in-law, and six grandchildren. Visit him at OSHawkins.com and follow him on X @OSHawkins.